Pushing at the frontiers of change

Pushing at the frontiers of change
A memoir of Quaker involvement with homosexuality

David Blamires

QUAKERbooks

First published March 2012
Quaker Books, Friends House, 173 Euston Road, London, NW1 2BJ.

ISBN 978-1-907123-23-8
© David Blamires, 2012

Cover design by Michael Preston
Book designed and typeset by Gaby Scott
Printed by Information Press
Set in Minion Pro

Britain Yearly Meeting is a registered charity, number 1127633.
Britain Yearly Meeting is committed to becoming a low-carbon, sustainable organisation. All our books are printed on FSC certified paper. FSC certified forests are managed with consideration for people, wildlife and the environment.

www.quaker.org.uk

Preface

After the *Friends Quarterly* published my article 'Writing Homosexuality from the inside'[1] in August 2010, it gradually became clear to me that now was the time to write a short account of British Friends' involvement in the various processes leading to homosexual equality. These processes had, after all, been going on since the late 1950s – a fact that many Friends today are unaware of. Most of this has taken place during my adult life, and I have been personally involved in a considerable amount of it. What I have written in the present book is a mixture of history and autobiography. Sometimes I use the pronouns 'I' and 'we', sometimes the more detached third person. I have allowed myself occasional personal comments, but I have tried to be fair to those with whom I disagree or have disagreed.

Most of those involved in the writing and publication of *Towards a Quaker view of sex: An essay by a group of Friends* (1963) have died, but fortunately the group's papers are held in the Library of Friends House, London. I have been grateful to have access to them. The chapter on *Homosexuality from the inside* first appeared in the *Friends Quarterly*, as indicated above. The first person to write about the beginning years of the Friends Homosexual Fellowship was Ben Pink Dandelion in a thesis entitled *The history of F.H.F., 1973–87* (1987), which is rich in factual information, particularly about the composition of the committee and the venues and topics of national gatherings. The archive of FHF is in Friends House

Library, but is not on open access. I have used my own personal papers for all matters concerned with FHF and the group that produced *This we can say* (1995).

Several friends have given me relevant papers and Xeroxed material as well as commenting on and correcting drafts of particular chapters. Their help has been enormously encouraging. I wish to thank especially the staff of Friends House Library for their cheerful responses to every request. Frank Boulton, Nick Chadwick, Ben Pink Dandelion, Jeremy Greenwood, Susan V. Hartshorne, Dot Hull, Michael Hutchinson, Alex Kerr, Ted Milligan, Elisabeth Salisbury, David Saunders, Matthew Schofield and Chris Skidmore have all been helpful in a variety of ways.

A number of abbreviations are used in the text as follows:

CHE = Campaign for Homosexual Equality

FHF = Friends Homosexual Fellowship

FHSC = Friends Home Service Committee

HFTI = Homosexuality from the inside

QHS = Quaker Home Service

QLGF = Quaker Lesbian and Gay Fellowship

QW = *Quaker Work* (i.e. part of *Documents in Advance* of Yearly Meeting)

TQVS = Towards a Quaker view of sex

TWCS = This we can say

YM = Yearly Meeting

YM Proc = Yearly Meeting Proceedings

YM Docs = Yearly Meeting Documents in Advance

Contents

For Bernard Ratigan

1

Towards a Quaker view of sex

I grew up during the 1940s and 50s, which was not an easy time for a boy very gradually discovering his homosexuality and coming to terms with the fact. Homosexuality was a taboo subject, very rarely spoken about and then only with disapproval. It was impossible to find any sources of information that were not shrouded with negative associations. Books that dealt with sexuality or sex education focused virtually exclusively on heterosexuality, but that too was hedged around with prohibitions on masturbation and pre-marital intercourse. Adolescent crushes were fitfully recognised, but as something that girls and boys were expected to grow out of. For both sexes the aim was marriage, and that was for life. Adultery led inevitably to divorce, which was rare. Pre-marital sex often involved shame and social problems. 'Forced' marriages were commonplace when a baby was on the way. This happened with a girl and a boy in my form at grammar school. As far as I can remember, the rest of us in the class were intrigued rather than shocked.

As for homosexuality, newspapers such as the *News of the World* seemed to specialise in reporting prosecutions of men for 'gross indecency', though gross indecency was never spelt out so it was threatening and scary. Large fines or even imprisonment followed, often with further consequences such as loss of employment, social ostracism and gloating publicity. Some men, often married, caught in this way committed suicide. The public and the police were generally unconcerned about the damage done to useful lives and relationships with other people. Antony Grey notes:

> Between 1945 and 1955 the number of annual prosecutions for homosexual behaviour rose from under 800 to just over 2,500, of whom over 1,000 were given custodial sentences. When cases came to court, men were frequently sent to prison for private consenting behaviour with other adults committed years before.[1]

The mid 1950s saw a number of books published that dealt with different aspects of homosexuality. One of them, *Against the law*, Peter Wildeblood's autobiographical account of his involvement in the high-profile prosecution of Lord Montagu of Beaulieu and four other men, was first published in 1955 by Weidenfeld & Nicolson and republished by Penguin Books in 1957. Also in 1955 Longmans, Green published Derrick Sherwin Bailey's *Homosexuality and the western Christian tradition*, and Duckworth published D.J. West's general study, *Homosexuality*, which was republished by Penguin Books in 1960. This coincidence of books from the autobiographical, Christian and criminological viewpoints can be interpreted as reflecting the unease at the treatment and virtual persecution of male homosexuals in Britain at this time. The fact that Penguin republished two of the books within a short period brought the matter to a wider range of the reading public.

The trial of Lord Montagu and four other men of different social backgrounds accused of homosexual offences had involved the two RAF men in the case turning Queen's Evidence. This in turn led to changes in public sympathies as the trial was reported in the press. There was widespread public dismay at how matters had been engineered. The trial's principal target was Lord Beaulieu, but several others were caught and badly injured in the process. Peter Wildeblood gives a sober, telling account of his own involvement in the case. Clearly, there were serious matters that needed to be addressed.

In August 1954 a Home Office departmental committee was appointed under the chairmanship of John Wolfenden, Vice-Chancellor of Reading University (from 1956 John Wolfenden). Its remit was

> to consider (a) the law and practice relating to homosexual offences and the treatment of persons convicted of such offences by the courts; and (b) the law and practice relating to offences against the criminal law in connection with prostitution and solicitation for immoral purposes, and to report what changes, if any, are in [their] opinion desirable.[2]

The fifteen-person committee reported in September 1957, but its recommendations were not translated into law until ten years later. The *Report* was a hot potato, and no government was ready to deal with it. It was shelved, but its contents began very slowly to make an impact on thinking, if not on police practice.

Such was the context for the beginnings of Quaker engagement with attitudes towards homosexuality. It was sparked off by problems among the body of Young Friends at Cambridge round about 1954–55. At that time Cambridge Friends Meeting at Jesus Lane had a large and lively group of Young Friends who gathered regularly on Sunday evenings during term-time at Anna Bidder's house for coffee and discussion. Anna Bidder (1903–2001) had a marvellous rapport with students, so it was natural for them to take their problems and ideas to her. In an article published in the October 1988 issue of the *Friends Quarterly* (of which I was at that time the editor) she described how *Towards a Quaker view of sex* came to be written. It was a lengthy process and five or six years passed before the booklet was eventually published in February 1963. As I was an undergraduate and postgraduate at Cambridge from 1954 to 1960, I had some idea that things were happening, but I was not involved in them in any way. It was not until I had left Cambridge in 1960 that I began to think of myself as homosexual. I had been in love with another man on three occasions before I realised that what I felt for them was what heterosexuals called love, and that my sexual orientation was homosexual.

The group of fellow Quakers that Anna Bidder brought together in 1957 consisted of eleven people with diverse complementary backgrounds. There were eight men and three women (the Wolfenden Committee also had three women, but twelve men). The qualifications of the individual members of the group were listed in the published booklet along with their names. In alphabetical order they were: Kenneth C. Barnes[3], Headmaster of Wennington School, Wetherby; Anna M. Bidder, Research Worker and Teacher in Zoology, Cambridge University; Richard Fox, Consultant Psychiatrist, Severalls Hospital, Colchester; Alastair Heron (1915– 2009), Fellow of the British Psychological Society; Director of the Rhodes-Livingstone Institute, Lusaka; G. Joyce James (1905–94)[4], Housewife, one-time Marriage Guidance Counsellor; Kenneth Nicholson, Headmaster, Friends' School, Saffron Walden; Mervyn Parry, Teacher of educationally subnormal children, one-time assistant housemaster in a borstal; Lotte Rosenberg, Consultant Psychiatrist and Child Psychiatrist; Alfred Torrie, Fellow of the British Psychological Society; Consultant Psychiatrist; Keith Wedmore, Barrister-at-Law. The member of the group that had to remain anonymous for professional reasons was Duncan Fairn[5], who was Director of the Prison Service in the Lord Chancellor's Office.

As has been the case with almost all of the initiatives aimed at improving the situation of homosexuals, this Quaker group was not an official committee of the Religious Society of Friends: it was a group of individuals who over time began to think of themselves as working under concern, that is, that they felt called to their task. Whether any of them had any personal involvement apart from responding to the Cambridge Young Friends' request for help, I do not know, but their various professions and other contacts clearly must have made them conscious of many of the problems facing homosexual people at this particular time.

The group met monthly at Anna Bidder's London club over a period of five to six years, beginning each time with worship and then proceeding to discussion of particular issues. Sometimes they met other groups of Quakers with concerns that overlapped with their own. Although their focus was homosexuality, they felt it important to place it in the broader context of sexuality in general. They were not primarily concerned with the legal issues that faced the Wolfenden Committee, but rather with personal relationships, morality and the social aspects of homosexuality. Nor were they overburdened by traditional understandings of homosexuality as found in the Old Testament and some Pauline epistles, which led most mainstream churches to negative and judgemental attitudes. In the minutes they made of their meetings they called themselves the Quaker Group on Homosexuality and Other Problems of Sex (it was unfortunate that a couple of male members of the group were heard referring jocularly to it as the Quaker Committee on Buggery). They first met with no expectation of publishing anything, but eventually they realised that they needed to write what ultimately became *Towards a Quaker view of sex*.

The group published a four-column statement of how far they had got in their discussions in *The Friend* (20 May 1960). In it they pointed out that they had met with representatives of Young Friends, Heads of Quaker Schools, the Marriage and Parenthood Committee, the Friends Temperance and Moral Welfare Union, the Penal Affairs Committee, the Guild of Friend Social Workers and other concerned Friends. Thus they were not working secretly, and their statement in *The Friend* makes it plain what their position was. A fortnight later (3 June) a long letter from William Creed inveighed against the group as focusing "a strong and disturbing tendency in the Society towards humanism". This was counterbalanced by a calm letter from Theo and Alice Tulley (10 June) welcoming the discussion of homosexuality and encouraging Friends to join the Homosexual Law Reform Society. Further support for the group came from Elsie and Angus Earnshaw (17 June). Another letter from William K. Robinson (same date) distinguishes between homosexual feelings and physical acts, implying acceptance of the former only. So much for Letters to the Editor. However, the issue of 24 June includes a report of a conference that the group held at Hampstead Meeting House on 10 June, which demonstrates once more its attempts at spreading knowledge of its work more widely. Incidentally, both the group's statement and the report of the conference are headed 'Towards a Quaker view of sex'.

The printed booklet was probably the most influential document published by British Quakers in the twentieth century, if one judges by the number of editions it went through and the number of copies printed. It contributed massively to keeping the Friends Bookshop financially afloat. But before it attained that degree of success it encountered considerable setbacks. The first edition of *Towards a Quaker view of sex* was published by the Friends Home Service Committee (the ancestor of the department now called Quaker Life) in February 1963. It was edited by Alastair Heron, was 75 pages long and cost 3s. 6d. The cover was a sober dark green, with the title placed on an unevenly shaped white blotch. The group had originally sought an independent publisher, but on not being able to find one they turned to the Friends Home Service Committee (FHSC), which readily obliged, having long had a policy of publishing papers on various subjects by concerned Friends.

Prior to publication, however, Kenneth Barnes's good relations with the BBC had led to a TV programme on *'Meeting Point'* on the Sunday evening before the Monday publication date. Anna Bidder and Kenneth Barnes were the two Friends interviewed. The result was twofold: first, there was huge publicity for the booklet, the like of which had not been produced by any previous Christian group, and secondly, there was a prolonged fracas among British Friends about the mode of publication. Many Friends were up in arms because they had known nothing about the existence of the booklet before seeing the television programme or reading about it in the newspapers in the following days. They had clearly not registered the information given in 1960 and noted above. They felt that the booklet ought to have been properly discussed among Friends beforehand. Some thought that it shouldn't have been published at all.

It can't be said that the Yearly Meeting welcomed it with open arms. Although homosexuality was the topic that had led to the formation of the group, it was to a large extent ignored in the letters published in *The Friend*, where the main focus was on heterosexual relationships. Several correspondents were shocked at the booklet's questioning of the traditional Christian understanding of sexual relationships. The idea that premarital sex was not always wrong and that a single act of adultery need not necessarily lead to divorce was profoundly disturbing to them. The booklet's authors, however, were not preaching the abandonment of morality, but rather a morality that embraced all aspects of relationship, not simply an inflexible tradition. Such ideas were not new, of course, but they were new in being aired in a religious context.

Towards a Quaker view of sex was given an extensive review in *The Friend* (15 February 1963) by John Ounsted, Headmaster of Leighton Park School, Reading. He insisted on facing reality, on the wrongness of taking sexual relationships casually and on the equality of the sexes. He said almost nothing specifically about homosexuality. In a way this was a proper reaction, as a major point of the booklet was its insistence on the basic similarity of homosexual and heterosexual emotional and moral experience, expressed as follows:

> Surely it is the nature and quality of a relationship that matters: one must not judge it by its outward appearance but by its inner worth. Homosexual affection can be as selfless as heterosexual affection, and therefore we cannot see that it is in some way morally worse.
>
> Homosexual affection may of course be an emotion which some find aesthetically disgusting, but one cannot base Christian morality on a capacity for disgust. Neither are we happy with the thought that all homosexual behaviour is sinful: motive and circumstances degrade or ennoble any act, and we feel that to list sexual acts as sins is to follow the letter rather than the spirit, to kill rather than to give life.
>
> Further we see no reason why the physical nature of a sexual act should be the criterion by which the question whether or not it is moral should be decided. An act which expresses true affection between two individuals and gives pleasure to them both, does not seem to us to be sinful by reason *alone* of the fact that it is homosexual.[6]

The mixed reaction of British Friends to *Towards a Quaker view of sex* (*TQVS*) is not completely surprising. Strong emotions were evoked on all sides, both positive and negative. The publicity generated by the television programme deflected much of the attention away from the content of the booklet onto the procedural issues of its publication. Henry L. Wilson, writing with naïve optimism to *The Friend* (22 February 1963) wished that the writers had had more patience, so that their work could have borne the imprint of the *whole* Society. In the same issue Rona Forsey questioned the practice of publishing the work of an unofficial group. Many other correspondents echoed that misgiving and various degrees of opposition. Mary S. Milligan (8 March) expressed her reservations more carefully, pointing out that small groups needed to share and pool their experiences and that time was required for the whole Society to come to terms with them.

Meanwhile, Meeting for Sufferings (the national executive body of Friends in Britain), meeting on 1 March, noted the distress of many Friends and asked FHSC to reconsider its procedure for sponsoring publications. This elicited a long minute from FHSC's General Committee held over the weekend of 5–7 April, in which it declared its position:

> It has long been our policy to publish over the imprint of the FHSC books and pamphlets written by individuals or groups. The publication of this essay (*Towards a Quaker view of sex*) is therefore no new departure in policy. Such publication is arranged by our Literature Committee, having obtained the judgment of at least two, and in this case three, responsible Friend readers. This judgment is upon the suitability of the document as well-written literature deserving publication. It has never been a censorship, which is what would result from any attempt to limit publication to statements with which all Friends would agree. We believe any such limitation would be wrong.

Towards a Quaker view of sex was widely reviewed in the popular press and serious newspapers and journals. Almost all the reviews and press accounts treated the booklet with admiration, but some of them were careless about its title and about the booklet's status within the Society of Friends. It was important to Friends that it should be made clear that this was not *the* Quaker view of sex, but the view of a group without any official standing. When the group met much later in the year to discuss revising the booklet to take account of various criticisms, they decided to maintain the original title with its 'Towards' and 'a Quaker view of sex'. As some Friends had feared, the ostensible safeguards of 'towards' and 'a' were still liable to fade away in the popular mind. George H. Gorman[7], the General Secretary of FHSC, was kept busy over a long period of writing to correct misapprehensions in some of the reviews and letters addressed to non-Quaker periodicals. A rumour even arose that a Quaker group somewhere was requesting the opening of a clinic to advise on birth control. Such false ideas had to be squashed.

Letters to *The Friend* continued for several weeks with between four and eight contributions each time. A considerable number applauded the booklet for its honesty and timeliness. Peter Reeman thought it should be read from beginning to end – or not at all, while Brian F. Bone deplored the over-quick critical letter writers (both 1 March). W. Harry Butler suspected that the immediate reaction of some Friends was based on unthinking and uncreative criteria. Judith Maddocks, a student at Nottingham University, provided welcome information about the impact of the booklet outside Friends (29 March):

> My copy of *Towards a Quaker* view of sex is now in the hand of a Roman Catholic student of this University. This is after it has been used in a discussion group of the Presbyterian and Congregational Society and in a discussion group on Christianity and Sex. It has been recommended in a psychology tutorial group and many students I know have bought copies of their own.

Much interest has been aroused by it within the student population and praise that something new and relevant should come out of the Christian Church. Certainly its publication has stimulated much lively discussion and, if for this reason alone, has been worth while.

While Friends continued to struggle with their responses to the booklet, the press in general sounded a more positive note. Jumping the gun in typical fashion about the television programme with Anna Bidder and Kenneth Barnes, the *News of the World* declared robustly:

One of the frankest-ever public discussions on sex and morals will be put out by BBC television during family viewing time tonight. It is based on a shock report by a group of Quakers who accept that the loss of virginity before marriage is no longer a stigma.

With its key words 'frankest-ever', 'during family viewing', 'shock report', 'loss of virginity' and 'stigma', the *News of the World* alerted its readers to a good story. Less emotively nailing her colours to the mast, Marjorie Proops, widely respected as an agony aunt, wrote in the *Daily Mirror* (18 February): 'it was like a breath of fresh, clean spring air listening to sensible people talking sense about sex and morality as set out in the report by eleven Quakers.' In *The Sunday Times* (24 February) Monica Furlong wrote a piece headed 'Why I'm on the side of the Quakers'. On the same day *The People* published an article by Kenneth Baily (who was actually a Quaker) under the heading 'Gone – this old image of the Quakers; Today in their ranks they have youngsters like these [photo of a young man and woman]. Who says they're killjoys now?'

The Tablet (23 February) gave the booklet a long, thoughtful review from a critical Catholic viewpoint, restating traditional teaching on love-making, the vocation to chastity and homosexuality. It concluded: 'Where a reading of this pamphlet, whatever its deficiencies of judgment, can be salutary for us is in reminding us of the dangers of a legalistic approach and of the letter that killeth rather than the spirit that quickeneth.'

The Times Literary Supplement (1 March) declared that the booklet was 'often muddle-headed and sometimes fails to see the fuller possible implications of what is being said.' The reviewer, not having taken on board the booklet's primary function, deplored 'the disproportionate space given to one problem, homosexuality – sixteen out of forty-three pages of text proper.' He/she also noted: 'Nothing whatsoever is said about the problems of contraception and abortion in relation to the increase...of sexual relations between adolescents and young people before marriage.'

The impact of *Towards a Quaker view of sex* was not confined to Britain: it was reviewed or noted in a variety of newspapers and religious journals in the Netherlands, Norway, Switzerland and the United States. Requests were received from Germany and Italy about possible translations, and there was also one from the Royal National Institute for the Blind about producing a Braille edition. What became of these requests I do not know, but without a shadow of doubt interest in the issues raised by the booklet spread quickly far beyond the narrow bounds of British Quakerism. It was read and studied in Britain and abroad, in other Christian bodies and by people without any religious affiliation. By November 1963 demand had been so great that it reached a sixth impression.

In the course of the controversy among Friends and the reactions from outside it became clear that the text of *TQVS* was in places ambiguous and misleading. Where this was the case people were prone to understand such passages in the worst possible way. Further disquiet among Quakers surfaced in Meeting for Sufferings on the first Friday of November when the matter was raised by the Clerk, Doris I. Eddington[8]. A statement was eventually agreed as follows:

> In view of recent publicity, Meeting for Sufferings, the Standing Representative Committee of the Society of Friends in Great Britain, desires to remove current misunderstanding arising out of the pamphlet entitled *Towards a Quaker view of sex*. Its authors, meeting privately, with no appointment from any official committee of the Society, attempted to face problems they had encountered professionally or in social investigation, and their conclusions, as set out in the pamphlet, are a valuable contribution to modern thinking. They have not been endorsed by the Society, which has reached no judgement on the social problems with which the essay is concerned. Though Friends generally recognise the need for deep understanding in considering the changing social patterns of a generation which is no longer consciously Christian, the Society of Friends reaffirms its basic belief in the sanctity of life long nature of marriage, in pre-marital chastity, and in fidelity within marriage as expressions of the Christian ideal.

The experienced student of Quaker minutes will recognise the careful wording of this minute and the tensions that reside within it and almost explode. A letter from George Gorman, General Secretary of FHSC, to Anna Bidder on 7 November illuminates certain aspects of it:

> I don't think any member of Meeting for Sufferings could exactly be proud of the meeting on Friday. If, however, anything was ever bulldozed through by a majority – it was that statement! However, I gather that Stephen Thorne[9]

has already passed onto Doris Eddington one violent protest about the way it was handled. You may be glad to know that the word "valuable" was added as a result of the discussion in Sufferings, and I think many people, for example, Myrtle Radley[10], would not have agreed to the statement being accepted without this adjective.

The statement was probably too late for it to make much impact on the general public, but it signalled to British Quakers that important elements in the Society were strongly opposed to the major thrust of *TQVS*. Again, we have to note that the statement of Meeting for Sufferings said nothing about homosexuality.

The question of revising the text of *TQVS* was now becoming acute. In the 22 March issue of *The Friend* Robin Hodgkin in an article entitled 'Why a New Morality?' had asked: 'Have the authors been too concerned with abnormal behaviour? Have they been over-influenced by psychological and sociological considerations at the expense of religious ones?' On 12 April 1963 Alastair Heron replied in some detail in *The Friend* to many comments and criticisms made about certain aspects of the booklet. Alastair, on behalf of the authors, accepted some of the criticism levelled at the booklet, especially where there was ambiguity in the text, as, for example, in the passage alluding to the so-called 'triangular situation' that might arise in heterosexual relationships. The authors had not envisaged that this would be taken as condoning adultery. The passage accordingly was removed from the revised edition. Criticism of the booklet, in Alastair's summary, centred on three issues: (1) undue emphasis on the person-to-person relationship; (2) rejection of the traditional Christian Churches' attitude to morality; and (3) ambiguity or vagueness of expression.

Separately from all this, George Gorman received an agitated letter from Hugh Doncaster[11], who was Reader in Quaker History at Woodbrooke, the Quaker college that was part of the Selly Oak

Colleges in Birmingham. In the letter, dated 1 November 1963, he asked for a change in the title, removing the word 'Quaker', and inveighed against the use of the letter E to indicate, in the list of co-authors, which individuals were elders of the Society of Friends. Hugh, reacting in hyperbolic terms, regarded it as an 'abuse of office and reprehensible to a degree unparalleled by anything I know of among Friends'. I assume that the co-authors used the innocent E to assure their readers that several of their number were responsible members of the Society and not a bunch of disaffected cranks. But they accepted Hugh's criticism, and the letter E was omitted in the revised edition.

While the revised edition, first issued in 1964, is substantially the same in content as the first edition, there are several omissions, additions and rearrangements of material. The critics of the first edition would have found much less to argue about. While maintaining the same price of 3s. 6d., the text was expanded from 75 to 84 pages. The group resisted any change to the title, but made it clear that the booklet was 'an essay by a group of Friends'. Alastair Heron's name was removed an editor, as he was not involved in the revision on account of his appointment to the Rhodes-Livingstone Institute in Lusaka. The group agreed not to include the statement issued by Meeting for Sufferings in November 1963.

The revision was thoroughgoing and detailed. Nonetheless, the core of the group's message remained very much the same, even though paragraphs and sections were moved about, some short passages omitted and others inserted. The revised edition continued to be reprinted until about 1990, by which time events had made it a historical rather than a relevant contemporary document. It was frequently listed as required reading for student courses in religion or sociology at university and college level. Its sober format seemed almost calculated for use as a textbook. Equally importantly, however, it provided help and support for many individual homosexual men and women who were anxious and unsupported in a society that did not value them. We have to remember that, despite the Wolfenden Committee's report in 1957, the laws against male homosexual behaviour remained on the statute book until 1967. Even when the law was finally changed and received the Royal Assent in July of that year, it did not stop other constraints on homosexual activities. The provisions of the new law were interpreted as narrowly as possible, so an atmosphere of anxiety and potential threat continued. As Antony Grey noted, increasing numbers of public indecency and importuning offences were reported to the Homosexual Law Reform Society,[12] indicating heightened police activity. Some members of the legal professions and the law-enforcement agencies continued for several years to fight a rearguard action against the new law.

The work that the members of the *TQVS* group had engaged in while producing their original edition had led to some changes in their own individual attitudes. They referred to this in the first edition: 'Some members of our group have found themselves compelled to surrender assumptions that they had long accepted as good and right, because the emphasis on morality has so often gone with a cold and inhibitive attitude.'[13] One might have thought that this statement would encourage readers of the booklet to a change in their own preconceived ideas, but it was omitted from the revised text.

The revision expands the section on 'Adolescence'.[14] To the section on 'The Single Man and Woman' it adds at the end: 'The majority of single men and women lead happy lives of great fullness. Some accept their state, others have chosen it. There is no more vivid testimony in our time to the riches that can come from chosen celibacy than that of the life of the late Pope John XXIII.' This addition was probably made in order to give recognition to the contribution of the many single, unmarried individuals who might consider themselves otherwise to come under unjust suspicion of being crypto-homosexual. The section on 'Marriage and Later

Life' opens with a long quotation from a pamphlet produced by the Marriage and Parenthood Committee of the Society of Friends, attempting to describe the nature of Christian marriage. This was not included in the first edition. The revised edition is much expanded. As mentioned earlier, the troublesome passage on the 'triangular situation' was removed.

The revised edition to some extent reorganises the order of the material in the chapter on 'Homosexuality'. It divides into sections what the first edition gave as continuous text. After a brief introduction we thus find sections entitled 'Male Homosexuality', 'The Early Twenties', 'Later Years', 'Male Homosexuality in Britain', 'Male Homosexuality and the Law' (the longest section), 'Female Homosexuality' and finally 'A Christian Attitude'. Necessarily, it is concerned with the position of homosexuals at the time, that is, from about 1955 to 1963, but if one takes that into account it makes many points that are useful today.

The co-authors of TQVS were mainly middle-aged professional men and women. Three of them were consultant psychiatrists, and two were Fellows of the British Psychological Society. Of the three involved in education, two were headmasters of boarding schools at secondary level and had experience of the kind of sexual problems facing adolescent boys and girls. Joyce James had long experience as a marriage guidance counsellor. Anna Bidder, whose professional qualifications were in academic zoology, had considerable understanding of student problems by virtue of being the unshockable recipient of many calls for help. Two men brought to the group different aspects of the legal profession, one from the bar, the other from the prison service at various senior levels. Clearly, they had between them a fund of professional experience of legal, social and personal problems relating to sex and sexuality. What they attempted to provide in TQVS was an objective, up-to-date, liberal Christian view of sexuality with a particular emphasis on homosexuality. Sensing the amount of ignorance in society about homosexuality and the social taboos on even talking about it (let alone writing), they saw their task at one level as to provide unprejudiced reliable information. They also felt it essential to place homosexuality within the context of sexuality in general.

The 1950s and 60s were a period of great questioning and change with regard to both sexual behaviour and Christian theology, so this small Quaker group had a lot to ponder on. They did not in fact have a trained Quaker theologian among them and were not concerned with debating the niceties of traditional Biblical views on homosexuality. Much of this had in any case been explored by Canon Derrick Sherwin Bailey in *Homosexuality and the western Christian tradition*.[15] Though the group appreciated his work, they were nonetheless ready to disagree with his view that 'I love you' never ought to be said unless marriage was possible. The group's position was firmly based in what we nowadays call pastoral theology, which is prepared to take issue with Biblical or dogmatic theology and to argue strongly against the universal validity of statements made in societies that had entirely different concepts of behaviour and value from ours two thousand or more years later.

To return now to the matter of the virtual lack of comment on homosexual issues by individuals expressing their opinions in *The Friend*, readers today may find this puzzling. Did Friends in 1963 ignore this part of *TQVS* in their shock or their excitement about what the co-authors said with regard to pre-marital sex among young heterosexuals? Did they block it from their consciousness? Or were they actually in general agreement with the co-authors' position? We might surmise perhaps that they had no experience in the matter and thus left it to one side. Alternatively, individuals may not have wished to compromise themselves by expressing approval in a situation where they could have faced reprisals from the law. No doubt all of these questions played a part.

Most people in campaigning groups are motivated by some personal connexion or experience. They are either directly affected themselves or they have a friend, acquaintance or relative who is so affected. As far as I am aware, few Friends were involved in campaigning for homosexual law reform at this period, though *The Friend*[16] noted that George Gorman was a member of the Honorary Committee of the Homosexual Law Reform Society. Perhaps the taboo on homosexuality in the wake of the Oscar Wilde trial of 1895 dampened Quaker involvement. It is possible also that the circumstances in which many individuals were brought before the law provoked disgust rather than pity and militated against campaigning for lenient treatment or reform of the law. At this distance in time it is easier to pose questions than to answer them. In the period from the early 1950s to 1967 there was a great mixture of attitudes towards homosexuality and individual homosexuals according to the religious and social background from which people came. Quakers were not different from the general population in the range of their views.

2

Writing *Homosexuality from the inside*

When I was a teenager in the early 1950s sexuality in general was a fraught subject. Certain newspapers such as the *News of the World* published coded reports on sexual aberrances, rarely being straightforward. Occasionally they would report court cases about men being prosecuted for public indecency and sent to prison or fined. In the process otherwise ordinary lives, responsibilities and careers would be summarily disrupted or destroyed. By the time I realised what my own emotions were telling me, I knew that from society's point of view it was illegal and could have serious consequences. But I'm glad to say that when I had my first physically expressed gay experience, it was so wonderful that I couldn't possibly think it was wrong. That was before the law was changed (in 1967) to permit sexual relations between consenting adult males in private.

When *Towards a Quaker view of sex* came out in 1963 it was a liberating experience not only for me, but for many, many Friends and other people in the Christian community and beyond. It came in the wake of the *Report of the Committee on Homosexual Offences and Prostitution*, usually known as the *Wolfenden Report* after the name of its chairman Sir John Wolfenden, which was presented to Parliament in September 1957. The Government did nothing about its recommendations on changes to the law in England and Wales until 1967.

Both before and after this date pressure groups of various kinds formed to move matters on. It was the time of Women's Liberation, Gay Liberation, the Campaign for Homosexual Equality (CHE), the first openly gay magazines in Britain, and so on. By and large historical accounts of this period have ignored the ferment in the churches and concentrated on the more flamboyant and aggressive tactics of gay rights activists. There were, nonetheless, many books and pamphlets written within the Christian churches including, for example, Derrick Sherwin Bailey's *Homosexuality and the western Christian tradition* (1955) and Norman Pittenger's *Time for consent* (1970).

I joined CHE in 1970. It had its national office in Kennedy Street, Manchester, and Paul Temperton, one of the two secretaries, was an attender at Mount Street Meeting. Some of the local CHE group meetings took place in the meeting house. There was also in Manchester a telephone counselling service (from the Quaker viewpoint rather confusingly called Friend) that I belonged to. Meanwhile I had also become a Monthly Meeting representative on Meeting for Sufferings and had been since 1965 one of the half-dozen British representatives on the Friends World Committee for Consultation (FWCC). This was all part of the context for the eventual production of *Homosexuality from the inside*.

How did it come about? There was a review in *The Friend* (7 May 1971) of Charlotte Wolff's book *Love between women* that elicited a good deal of correspondence. One contribution seemed to me so wrong-headed that I asked the editor if he would accept an anonymous article putting an inside view of the subject of homosexuality. I wanted it to be anonymous because I had not told my mother about my homosexuality and did not want to upset her by coming out publicly at this juncture. The editor agreed, and the result was an article entitled 'Homosexuality from the inside'[1].

Following this I received, via the obliging editor of *The Friend*, many letters from Friends, both men and women, elderly, middle-aged and young, expressing their appreciation of what I had written. Several of them poured out their sense of relief at being able to share their experience, to know that there were other people out there who were in a similar position to themselves and would understand. It became clear that the situation could not simply be left there; something else had to be done. I already had support from a number of Friends in Manchester and Cambridge. Damaris Parker-Rhodes[2] had been on an extended visit to California, talking to Quakers about sex, drugs and mysticism, and offered her home in Cambridge for a small group to meet in late October and mull over what we might do next, perhaps a revision of *Towards a Quaker view of sex*. The article in *The Friend* was a beginning, but we felt, given the widespread ignorance about homosexuality among Friends, that there was a need for a more extensive publication on the subject.

I can't remember exactly who was present on this occasion, but it certainly included Irene Jacoby (1930–98), her partner Hilary Beynon, Damaris and myself. Irene and I had got to know each other well when we went on a four-person Young Friend delegation to the Soviet Union in 1959, but we did not know then that the other was homosexual. It is galling not having a clear memory of this crucial gathering, as it resulted in the decision for me to write a more extensive draft piece, building on the article in *The Friend* and our Cambridge discussion. Another step was for Irene and myself to meet with Arthur White[3] (Recording Clerk of London Yearly Meeting), George Gorman (General Secretary of Friends Home Service Committee) and Ted Milligan (of Friends House Library) to investigate possible sponsorship of the project. It later became clear that this would more readily fall within the remit of the Social Responsibility Council (SRC).

I was very aware that various American Quaker groups were concerned about similar matters. I had met Ron Mattson at a

Triennial Meeting of FWCC held in Sigtuna, Sweden, in the summer of 1970. As well as keeping me in touch with developments in the US, he invited me to stay with him in Minneapolis over the Christmas/New Year period 1971–72, and that was where I wrote the first draft of the *Homosexuality from the inside* booklet. While most of that visit was spent in Minneapolis, we also went to Pendle Hill for a New Year conference, and I got to meet some other gay Friends in the Philadelphia area, namely Geoffrey Kaiser and Bruce Grimes.

Anybody who has ever been a clerk or national committee member in Britain knows that Friends love to get their teeth into drafts, whether minutes, Yearly Meeting epistles or other Quaker documents. *Homosexuality from the inside* (*HFTI*) went through five drafts before actually being published. It was an excellent process. We were supported throughout by SRC, especially Leslie Smith (General Secretary) and his indefatigable secretary Polly Warner, who did an enormous amount of typing and retyping drafts for us and smoothed our path in other ways.

I am not sure just who participated in the meetings that we had through 1972 to consider the drafts and make improvements. We were not an appointed committee, but rather a group of Friends who were deeply concerned to provide Quakers (in the first instance) with a picture of what it felt like to be homosexual in the social circumstances of the time. It was a task that we felt was laid on us, a concern in the full Quaker sense of the term. The core group met at the Friends International Centre. Each draft in turn was shared with an increasing number of Friends, and we gained enormously from their suggestions and careful reading. Towards the end of our work we consulted with members of the group that had produced *TQVS* in 1963.

The text that we eventually presented to SRC for publication had undergone a lot of changes from what I had typed out in Minneapolis. That first draft was written in 48 numbered sections for ease of reference. The subject-matter survived overwhelmingly intact, and many passages in the published text are virtually identical with what I first wrote. However, we made many alterations, clarifying the meaning, dividing long sections into smaller paragraphs, re-ordering the material, adding occasional explanations and cutting out some passages. The main criticisms that we received focused on repetition and tone. Many of our readers found parts of the original hectoring and strident in tone and thus off-putting. This was very much the product of the time, especially of the Gay Liberation movement. Gay activists, impatient with the patriarchal attitudes of heterosexual society, wanted radical and immediate change, and they made an impact on more cautious Quakers.

The first draft ran the risk of alienating potential readers not only by its tone, but also by raising a number of contentious issues that diverted attention from our central objective, which was to raise general awareness of some of the difficulties that homosexual people experienced in contemporary society. A few examples may illustrate the changes that we made. The first draft contained a section heading 'The oppressive society', which was changed in the published text to 'The Pressures of Society'. The original draft's criticisms of some actions of the police, for example, in the entrapment of men in public toilets, were minimised, and remarks on intergenerational sex and the possibility of adolescents egging on adults were removed. More interesting from the viewpoint of Britain Yearly Meeting's 2009 decision at York regarding equality of gays and straights in respect of marriage is the fact that the original draft had five numbered sections headed 'Homosexual marriage'[4]. This was almost entirely omitted from the published text, which states evasively instead: 'There are, of course, many implications and problems arising from any idea of homosexual marriage and this is not the place to go into them'[5].

It is perhaps worth spending a little more time on this. The situation in the United States, with State as well as Federal law, was well in advance of the United Kingdom. Section 40 mentions 'the attempt of Jack Baker and Michael McConnell to have their relationship – they were married by a Methodist pastor – recognised by the State of Minnesota as a marriage on the same legal basis as the marriage of heterosexual couples.' This was a *cause célèbre* at the time, and there have been many similar cases since then with many States permitting homosexual marriages, while others explicitly prohibited them. I'm not quite sure when American Yearly Meetings started writing minutes in support of gay marriage, but at least three of them did quite early on, namely, Pacific, Philadelphia and New York.

But to return to the first draft, sections 40–44 looked in detail at the religious or spiritual aspect of marriage as well as the social and legal aspects. There were references to *Church Government*[6] and the importance of the *public* declaration of the couple desiring to be married. Section 44 stated: 'The Society of Friends, or any other branch of the Christian church, might well be willing to bless the union of two men or two women and recognise this as a marriage from the religious point of view, but this would not be satisfactory if that couple still did not enjoy the same benefits and privileges accorded to male-female couples.'

I have no clear memory of the precise reasons for omitting all of this from the published text of *Homosexuality from the inside*, but I suspect that members of SRC felt that to include it would damage the prospects of the central issues of the booklet being properly addressed. With the benefit of hindsight, I think they were right, but the draft's arguments are astonishingly close to the spirit of the Yearly Meeting Gathering's decision in 2009 in York.

The Social Responsibility Council having agreed to publish *HFTI*, it appointed Ted Randall to speak to the matter at Meeting for Sufferings at its meeting on 4 November 1972. This was prudent, as when *TQVS* was published it took many Friends completely by surprise, as the first they knew about it was through a television programme or the next day's newspaper. SRC did not want a repetition of this shock-horror reaction. It did, however, raise a problem for me, as I was myself a member of Meeting for Sufferings and I rather resented the fact that I was asked not to attend the meeting. Arthur White, the Recording Clerk (and incidentally a good personal friend), whose wise counsel I valued on many an occasion, wrote very carefully about this to me. His final sentence, 'Your absence, that is to say, could be very weighty in forwarding your concern' (letter dated 27 October 1972), proved to be triumphantly correct.

I did not attend Meeting for Sufferings, but ten days later I received a summary of its consideration compiled by Ted Milligan from Arthur White's notes. Some fifteen Friends spoke from a variety of viewpoints, both affirming and querulous and concerned that the booklet should not be understood as the statement of an official Quaker position. At least ten of the speakers knew me personally and were very supportive. Minute 6 of the meeting recorded, rather blandly: 'Ted Randall[7], speaking on behalf of Social Responsibility Council, has told us of the concern of a small group of homosexuals, men and women, mainly Friends, to produce a pamphlet on "Homosexuality from the inside", to be written by David Blamires. The Social Responsibility Council has approved this essay as a valuable contribution to the consideration of a subject of social importance. They recommend its publication as a document which should help towards a deeper understanding of a very sensitive problem; we accept this recommendation and encourage the Council to go forward.' In his covering letter Ted Milligan added: 'I forgot to tell you that when, in the minute, it was proposed to insert the words "both men & women" after "a group of homosexuals," Ted Randall found it hard to restrain himself from saying that the addition would be justified "as this is an instance where the male does not embrace the female".'

Not long after this I received a typically encouraging letter from

Bessie Blackburn (Elizabeth K. Blackburn) of Crawshawbooth Meeting (10 December 1972): 'I must say my heart was warmed when I heard that you were going to write this booklet – so sorely needed – and I want to say I am with you. I have met a number of Homosexuals (men & women) in the Civil Service and number three amongst my friends – and I have shared some of their difficulties, particularly of one, who was for a time my assistant. – But they have certainly made their contribution – and I have been enriched by knowing them.'

The climate of the time during which *HFTI* was worked on was such that no one on the group apart from myself felt easy about putting their name to the booklet. It was a time of uncertainty in which people were anxious about the possibility of losing their jobs because of coming out. This was particularly true of people who were teachers and civil servants in contact with members of the public. Although the law had been changed to permit a closely limited expression of homosexual desire in private, there was no legislation as yet to protect gay people's human rights. Several Friends felt anxiety on my behalf, and both Meeting for Sufferings and the published booklet referred to my courage in putting my name as author of *HFTI*. It didn't feel as heroic as that to me. The University of Manchester was a pretty safe place to work, and when I told the two Professors in the German Department that the booklet was about to be published and there might well be media interest, they were both supportive and said that it would not affect my position in the Department. I knew also that I had the solid support of Friends House, especially Leslie Smith, Arthur White and Ted Milligan, and of many Friends up and down the country and in other parts of the Quaker world. I did not feel that I was on my own.

As I look back at the booklet from the perspective of 2009, I'm aware of several things. The style of *Towards a Quaker view of sex* was modelled on a Civil Service document, and to a lesser degree *Homosexuality from the inside* followed the same pattern. The final text was deliberately sober. I remember that a woman Friend remarked to me how clever I was to have written it in such a dry way. That felt like a back-handed compliment. I'm also aware how little there is in the booklet about women. That is perhaps explicable because writing by lesbians was thin on the ground in the early 1970s and because I was writing as a gay man. In many ways lesbians felt closer to the aims of the women's movement than to gay liberation, in which men were the driving force. But I'm sorry that the language of *HFTI* was not more inclusive; there are an awful lot of he(s) around rather than he and she(s). In addition I regret that there was not more about the range and fluidity of sexual experience, about bisexuality and transgender issues. But to have included a more adequate consideration of these topics as well as interpretation of the Bible would have resulted in a book rather than a booklet, and probably fewer readers.

Homosexuality from the inside was published on 9 March 1973 in an edition of 10,000, price 20 pence. It was vi + 45 pages long. It consisted of a Foreword by Chris Barber and Leslie A. Smith, Chairman and Secretary respectively of SRC. Then followed an Introduction and short sections on attitudes towards homosexuality; sexual roles and orientation; the pressures of society; the process of self-discovery; the formation of relationships; conclusion; further reading; addresses of organisations. My brother designed the cover.

After publication I immediately started getting correspondence. By 4 May 1,635 copies of the booklet had been sold. There was a very sober, helpful review by Alfred Braithwaite[8] in *The Friend* (9 March). This was followed by the expected flow of Letters to the Editor; a few Friends blew their tops, but by and large the correspondence was encouraging. A small group calling themselves the Friends of Paul were antagonistic, but they quietened down after a time and faded away. There was a review in *The Guardian* (also 9

March), *Gay News* (no. 20), *Lunch* (another gay magazine, April), *Young Quaker* (April), *British Weekly / Christian Record* (6 April), *Reform* (the magazine of the United Reformed Church, June), *The Catonsville Roadrunner* (no. 44, by Judy Holding) and a note in the SMG (Scottish Minorities Group) Newsletter. There may well have been others that I don't know about.

The letters I received were extraordinarily varied. Some correspondents wrote at considerable length about their own stories of isolation, pain, frustration, their blighted lives. There were both men and women, the whole age range, as far as I could tell. Many were, of course, fellow Quakers or had Quaker connexions. Others came through wider publicity and found my address in diverse ways. These letters were not restricted to gay people. I had appreciative letters from many heterosexual Friends, from people who knew me from childhood or teenage days, from Friends whom I'd got to know through Quaker committees, Woodbrooke and locally. It was incredibly exhilarating. I'll try to give a snapshot of the kind of things I received.

Honor Butlin, a close friend and constant supporter of Rachel Pinney's work on Creative Listening, sent me a telegram (10 March 1973) with the simple but telling words 'Greetings greetings love Honor'. The Manchester University Librarian lost no time in writing (12 March 1973): 'Many thanks for the two copies of *Homosexuality from the inside* which you have so kindly presented to the Library. It is good to see such a misunderstood subject presented in an enlightened and humane way. I am certain it will be widely appreciated'. My dear friend Léonce Richards, who lent me a variety of German books in my teenage years, wrote from Keswick (20 March): 'Just a quick line to pay tribute to your courage and integrity and to put it to you, to try and not be hurt by some of the more virulent unquakerly outbursts in the correspondence column of *The Friend*'. I had a lovely letter from Alfred Stone of Ashton-on-Mersey meeting (now Sale) (9 March 1973), at the end of which he wrote: 'You will inevitably for some months be looked upon particularly as "the author of that book". This may at times be a strain, and I trust you will feel the thoughts of your wellwishers to be a support. Again, many thanks.'

One of the great pleasures of the correspondence was receiving letters out of the blue from people I had known well, but lost touch with. I will quote from one, leaving out names for obvious reasons:

> Dear David – <u>I am presuming that there is only one David Blamires</u>. Greetings – I am glad that 'SRC' has agreed to publish 'your' essay on "Homosexuality from the inside" and I would be pleased to know when it is published for I would very much like to see a copy. You will guess why if you can remember back far enough (apart from a professional interest)! – I still work as a Social worker with a bias to mental health problems...Despite all I've now been married for 7½ years and have 3 Kiddywinks...and enjoy being married.

Among other things, this letter illustrates the fact that being married was one of the reasons for some people being cautious or worried about what they could say about their gay experience.

Almost all the letters that I received after the publication of *HFTI* were positive. People who sounded off in a condemnatory way in *The Friend* usually did not know me personally. I had agreed to take part in a Religious Books Conference at Spode House, near Rugeley, at the end of January 1973, and a publisher, Inter-Varsity Press, sent me a copy of *The returns of love* by 'Alex Davidson' (a pseudonym). I found the book completely unacceptable and said in my reply to the publisher that I thought it would do considerable emotional damage to such troubled homosexuals as might read it (letter dated 22 January 1973).

I do not propose to deal any further with the reactions of the Friends of Paul, but I would like to mention a six-page letter that I had from an evangelical Friend whom I knew personally and who read the essay as 'a heart-cry for understanding from a soul who is fettered and bound'. She exclaimed: 'Oh David humble yourself and allow the Lord Jesus Christ to take control of you. He is the only One who can satisfy all your longings and desires. It is not a myth, He really satisfies and sets free. I know because He has set me free. He is worthy of our love. He is real. He is alive to day. Call upon Him. He will hear.' It was a deeply personal, sincere letter, not written in a censorious spirit, though it was one that I had to disagree with. In my reply (8 April 1973) I said: 'It would seem to me that from the Christian point of view what matters in a sexual relationship is the degree of tenderness and mutual caring shown in it. ...I know of several homosexual partnerships of long standing where the two people concerned are deeply strengthened and supported in their relationship in doing things of a truly spiritual and Christianly committed nature. I would venture to say that their lives are as dedicated as I know your own to be.' Although the evangelical Friend and myself took different positions on homosexuality, we respected, liked and got along well with each other for the next twenty-five years. She did not have a closed mind on the subject; far from it.

The correspondence in the wake of the publication of *HFTI* made clear without any shadow of doubt that there was a need for gay support groups and for befriending individuals who wanted to talk about their problems on a one-to-one basis. In the London area an organisation called Integroup, founded by the Unitarian minister Tony Cross, had been in existence since around 1970, possibly earlier, with groups in Catford and Golders Green. Later there was another group called Group 1000, so called because, with 5 per cent of the population estimated as being gay, there could be as many as 1000 gay Quakers. Angus Earnshaw (1924–2010)[9] was the moving force behind this group. Sybil Abbott of Westminster Meeting, a retired heterosexual Friend, provided a welcome venue at her flat near Friends House. Many gay Friends of both genders have reason to be grateful to Angus and Sybil for their generous friendship and hospitality.

Yearly Meeting provided the first opportunity after the publication of *HFTI* for gay Friends to meet together. Angus Earnshaw invited people to meet at his house in north London about 8.15 p.m. after the Swarthmore Lecture on Saturday, 26 May 1973; (this was *The amazing fact of Quaker worship* by George Gorman). We were also interested to find out what the prospect was for a one-day gathering or a weekend conference at a later date. On 2 July I was able to write to invite people to a conference over the weekend of 7–9 September at Hulme Hall, a men's Hall of Residence at the University of Manchester. The Warden of Hulme Hall was John Hartshorne[10], Clerk of Manchester Preparative Meeting, and he and his wife Susan made us very welcome. The agenda was a simple framework for us to get to know each other. Three general topics were suggested: (1) What are the problems of being gay? (2) Towards a moral code for gays; (3) Where to next? There were meetings for worship to begin each day, discussion groups, outings and social times. The cost was £6. Twenty-three attended the conference, of whom only five were women.

The main result of the gathering was the decision to found what we eventually called the Friends Homosexual Fellowship (FHF). From the start FHF welcomed sympathetic heterosexuals, but it was principally for homosexual Friends and attenders along with their friends or partners. Because at this stage in the development of the gay movement there were very few groups with a religious or spiritual dimension to them, a number of people came along who had little or no connexion with Quakers. As was the case with the telephone counselling service Friend, FHF found that many people contacted us in the hope that they might find a prospective partner, which did of course happen. The aims of FHF were as follows:

1. To encourage fellowship, friendship and support between members, and, where needed, to help those who have difficulty in coming to terms with themselves and others. To this end we encourage the formation of local groups for social activities and discussion.
2. To promote a dialogue within the Society of Friends at all levels, with a view to achieving a deeper mutual understanding.
3. To liaise with other homosexual groups, particularly those with a religious basis.

It is our belief that the Quaker idea of religion encompasses all aspects of life, and basic to this is the testimony that that of God is to be found in all people, not just those currently socially acceptable.

We are concerned that homosexuals, and others, be treated according to their humanness and not by any label attached to them. We claim a right to be heard and accepted for our humanness, and this makes us look forward to the day when the Fellowship can be laid down.

Michael Hutchinson was appointed as secretary, myself as chairman and Irene Jacoby as treasurer. The annual subscription was £1.00 (£1.50 for couples) payable to 'Friends Fellowship', NOT 'Friends Homosexual Fellowship'. This latter point illustrates the anxiety of many people at the time about declaring themselves as homosexual or being outed when they were not prepared for it. The Gay Liberation Movement exerted a lot of pressure on gay people, particularly those in positions of public prominence, to come out. FHF was very cautious about this and found it intimidatory and disrespectful of individuals' privacy. Although

FHF as a corporate body wanted to reach out to others, there were a number of individuals who, for quite a long time, had anxieties about identifying themselves or even going to gatherings on Quaker premises where they might be identified. There were understandable reasons for this. Not only was there worry about job-security, which was very real for teachers and others, but also many members of FHF were concerned about the hurt they might cause their parents or, in the case of married people, their spouses and children.

Michael Hutchinson was the person on whom much of the early work of FHF devolved and who did it with great commitment and sensitivity. Other members of the Fellowship contributed in less onerous ways. The writing of *HFTI* certainly changed my life. Even today people say discreetly to me, 'I've read your book,' and assume that I know it's *HFTI* that they're talking about. I too assume that Friends know that I wrote this, but that's only the case where they have been Friends for a long time. The majority of today's Friends have very little knowledge of even recent Quaker history and are unaware of the fact that in some shape or form Friends have been involved in gay rights issues for over fifty years. Very little of this took place within the official structures of the Yearly Meeting; it was mainly, in the first instance, a matter of small, unofficial groups working under concern and later sharing their experience with the wider body of Friends.

Quakers as a corporate body have been hesitant about getting involved with gay rights and issues to do with sexuality. After *TQVS* was published, Meeting for Sufferings, propelled by its Clerk, Doris I. Eddington, dissociated itself from the book, as noted earlier. Strikingly, though, the revision of *Quaker faith & practice* (agreed 1994, published 1995) contains an inclusive, ground-breaking chapter on 'Close relationships'. FHF itself had published a substantial, fine collection of individual testimonies, mainly by named individuals, as *Meeting gay Friends*, edited by

John Banks and Martina Weitsch[11]. More recently, FHF's successor, the Quaker Lesbian and Gay Fellowship (QLGF), published a comparable volume entitled *Part of the rainbow* (2004). Motivated by a personal concern for equality of treatment within the Society of Friends, Susan Hartshorne, as long ago as 1987, produced for Meeting for Sufferings materials for celebrating gay partnerships within Quaker meetings. The decision at Yearly Meeting 2009 at York should therefore be seen in the context of some fifty years of patient work by individuals and groups for equal treatment of homosexuals and heterosexuals.

After the publication of *HFTI* I received a lot of requests to give talks to a large number of Quaker bodies – local and area meetings, the Woodbrooke student group's Meeting Point, and so on. There was intense interest at the FWCC Triennial at Sydney, Australia, in August 1973, centring on a large informal gathering after the rest of the day's business was done. I had a special invitation to visit Friends in Brisbane, which resulted in my meeting Roger Sawkins, a three-month stay with him and his family shortly afterwards, and a still continuing friendship. I met others in Sydney who were involved in the gay movement, was interviewed on radio and met Dennis Altman, the author of *Homosexual oppression and liberation*[12]. Coincidentally, Dennis had been educated at Friends School, Hobart, Tasmania, the only Quaker school in Australia. David Hodgkin of Canberra Meeting did a review of *HFTI* for *The Australian Friend* and got 100 copies shipped out to Australia. The booklet circulated widely among Friends in the unprogrammed tradition in the USA and Canada. I also received an invitation to speak to German Friends, who were much challenged by Martina Weitsch's coming out.

All of this took place within a world-wide Quaker context, but there were developments in academia too. At Manchester University I was invited to speak to a group of colleagues who were involved in chaplaincy, pastoral and counselling work, among whom was Margot Young, Senior Lecturer in the French Department and Adviser to Women Students. Ronald Preston, who became first Professor of Pastoral Theology at the University, was also appreciative of *HFTI*. A number of male and female gay colleagues tried to get an informal gay studies programme going, but it did not take off. During the 1970s Manchester University was still a conservative, rather hide-bound institution. I did not personally experience any negative reactions from colleagues or students. In fact, there was a strong sense of mutual support, particularly between gay colleagues, but also generally whatever people's sexual orientation.

Because my name became well known I was often asked to write articles or give talks outside Quaker circles. Tony Dyson (A. E. Dyson), who was indefatigable in gaining support for homosexual law reform, asked me to contribute to the magazine *Christian*, for which I wrote 'Homosexuality and the Church: the case for honesty' (Annunciation 1977). This whole issue of the magazine was controversial. The editors and the editorial board were sharply divided, and the magazine eventually folded. I also contributed some reviews to the magazine *Lunch*, an offshoot of London CHE, which produced 24 issues between 1971 and 1973. One final footnote: *HFTI* was translated into French by Philippe Giron and published as a special number of ILIA with the title *L'Homosexualité telle que nous la vivons*[13]. Jonathan Fryer contributed an *avant-propos* about Quakers, and 2,500 copies were printed.

One of the remarkable things about writing books and articles is that they may have unanticipated afterlives. They may lie dormant or neglected for years, even decades, but then come to life again. The circumstances will no doubt be different and place the original publication in a changed context. Most of what I've written about here took place thirty-five years ago. For the broad outline I have relied on memory, but I have been to check most of it against a considerable personal archive of letters received and sent, diaries, copies of documents, newspaper and magazine cuttings. The immediate impetus for my re-engagement with these themes stems from a conversation I had with Matthew Schofield and an invitation to speak to a meeting of QLGF in autumn 2009. Parts of this chapter, however, were embryonic in a talk that I gave to Quakers Uniting in Publications (QUIP) at Glenthorne, Grasmere, in April 2007[14]. It is a little odd being a historian of part of your own life, but the events I have written about have had lasting consequences.

3

Friends Homosexual Fellowship

Friends Homosexual Fellowship (FHF) was probably the first of the British unofficial Christian gay groups off the ground, run by those who belonged to it, and not sponsored by any of the various denominations. It did not stay the only such group for long. Other Christian groups sprang up – Baptist, Methodist, Congregationalist, Roman Catholic (called Quest), Unitarian, the Gay Christian Movement (which wanted to be ecumenical, but was principally Anglican) and Reach (which was evangelical). FHF was in touch with many of these groups, either through the clerk or assistant clerk or through individual personal links. FHF, however, was not inclined to become part of an ecumenical group, as our Quaker identity, liberal theology and way of doing things were paramount.

Within British Quakers generally there were some people who hoped that the formation of FHF would be just a temporary matter and that FHF would prove to be unnecessary as gays were accepted in society. They had probably not thought very deeply about the social and religious problems that gays faced or the capacity of traditionally minded Quakers themselves to change and adapt. Despite the fact that the law had been changed in 1967 with regard to male homosexual behaviour (there had never been a law against female homosexuality), this was merely the beginning as far as social attitudes were concerned. FHF had a lot on its plate to deal with, and it would take time. First, there was the matter of helping and supporting individual gay Friends and creating solidarity and self-confidence. Secondly, we needed to provide reliable information for Quakers about male and female homosexuality. Thirdly, we wanted to be part of the process of removing the injustices and discrimination that gays suffered in society at large.

These were big issues, and we could not attack them all at once. In any case, many other groups had arisen from the early 1960s to tackle the problems or particular aspects of social inequality. FHF's activities were influenced by the women's movement and the gay rights movement as well as fundamental questions that were being raised in radical religious circles. Germaine Greer's *The Female Eunuch* had been published in 1970. John A. T. Robinson, Bishop of Woolwich, produced *Honest to God* in 1963. Norman Pittenger's *Time for consent: a Christian's approach to homosexuality* was first published in 1967, with a second and third, revised and enlarged edition in 1970 and 1976. In 1971 Dennis Altman published *Homosexual oppression and liberation*[1], and in the autumn of the same year there broke onto the scene the *London Gay Liberation Front Manifesto*, produced collectively by a group. Jack Babuscio's *We speak for ourselves: experiences in homosexual counselling*[2] was also liberating for many people. Given that many of the problems confronting gays in the 1960s and 70s have their origin in stories and statements found in the Bible, it is strange that the struggles of religious groups in this period have been largely airbrushed out of historical accounts.

The number of individuals in FHF was small, but it gradually grew. It was more successful in remaining a mixed group of men and women than most of the other gay groups of the time. That was undoubtedly on account of our Quaker historical experience from at least the beginning of the twentieth century. Unlike other denominational groups, we did not have the weight of a male clerical hierarchy to contend with. The proportion of women to men was around a third. On occasion we would have women-only or men-only discussion groups for topics that were of particular interest to one sex, but for the most part we were happy to meet together. There were, of course, many gay Friends, both male and female, who chose not to become part of FHF. The paucity of other gay groups, particularly outside the Greater London area and particularly groups with a religious affiliation, meant that FHF was frequently approached by people with no Quaker connexion. This occasionally happened because of an understandable confusion with the gay telephone counselling service called Friend. Some people as a result became interested in Quakerism as well as the friendly support that FHF offered, while others after a time dropped out.

As well as organising other gatherings similar to the conference at which FHF was founded in September 1973, we had to draft a constitution. The process took until April 1975. The aims have already been given in the chapter on *Homosexuality from the inside*. Membership was to be open to (i) all members of the Society of Friends, (ii) attenders at Friends' meetings, (iii) the partners of members of the fellowship and (iv) non-Friends accepted after discussion with a committee member or member of the fellowship appointed to do so on the committee's behalf. Sexual orientation was not prescribed; heterosexual members were an important part of FHF from the start. We decided that the officers were to be clerk, assistant clerk, treasurer, conference organiser, counselling organiser and publicity organiser. The committee also had the power to co-opt and usually did so.

From the beginning FHF followed traditional Quaker procedures in holding meetings for worship and accepting minutes during business meetings. Because members felt more relaxed and self-confident in expressing themselves, sometimes for the first time in a group, the atmosphere of conference and discussion groups was often more open and candid than in many other situations. The concluding meetings for worship were frequently very profound experiences, not easily matched in one's own local meeting.

Each year we planned a residential weekend gathering and also a day conference somewhere in London. We were fortunate in being allowed to meet on a number of occasions at the Royal Foundation of St Katharine in Stepney, where we were made very welcome. London was the most convenient location because it was the focus of the national railway system, and members from all parts of the country could get there easily. But there were problems about cost (also faced by Meeting for Sufferings). Members living in the Greater London area were at a considerable advantage over those who lived at a distance, so we attempted to even things out by a pooled fare system, but it was not easy to administer. Over the years conferences were held at a large number of other centres including Damascus House, Mill Hill, All Saints Pastoral Centre, London Colney, Hengrave Hall, Bury St Edmunds, Charney Manor, Sheffield and Chorley.

To begin with we spent a lot of time listening to each other's experience of being gay, of discovering the nature of our sexuality, of coming out or not as the case might be. Some were or had been married and had children as well as spouses to consider. Some lived alone and were desperately lonely. Others had experienced problems of intolerance or rejection. Several men had lived the major part of their lives in the knowledge that they might be prosecuted, shamed and sent to prison. Through sharing our life-stories we could lessen our feelings of isolation and being different. For many the relief in finding others like themselves was palpable. Individuals coming to Quakerism from other denominations found a kind of freedom among us. On the other hand, some who had been brought up in a sober Quaker family often had deep feelings of guilt and failure to overcome.

Michael Hutchinson, our Assistant Clerk, and I personally

continued to receive letters from men and women distressed by the impact of their sexuality on their lives. Some in their naivety or desperation hoped that we could find a partner for them. We were thus starkly confronted with a vast need for pastoral care and support. Sympathetic listening was being sought, but it was clear that in many areas of Quakerism there was more ignorance than sympathy to be found. I say 'ignorance', but it could also have been intolerance or disapproval. Two of our members were told they were unwelcome at their meeting. It caused them acute distress and made FHF realise how difficult our task might be; not only for them but also for the majority of members FHF was a source of moral, emotional and spiritual support. It was a community of acceptance and encouragement where no one needed to hide.

The Gay Liberation Front believed passionately that it was necessary for gay people to 'come out' and identify themselves, and they did this flamboyantly. Needless to say (but I'm still saying it), it wasn't most Friends' style. We recognised, however, that if Friends were to be roused from their corporate ignorance FHF and its individual members needed to be more public. The more individuals 'came out', the easier it would be for Friends to treat gays as 'us' and not as a separate, somewhat dubious and distant 'them'. But it wasn't an easy option. Social pressures and personal worries often stood in the way. Nonetheless, it began to happen, and as FHF became more confident about holding gatherings in Quaker meeting houses, ignorance was gradually dispersed.

As far as official British Quakerism was concerned (it was then called London Yearly Meeting), the process began with special interest groups held during the Yearly Meeting period. These provided opportunities for sympathetic non-gay Friends to show their support and for tentative gay Friends to explore and put their feet in the water. Yearly Meeting Agenda Committee asked Irene Jacoby and Jeremy Greenwood to speak about their personal experience of homosexuality at a special interest group at the residential Yearly Meeting held at the University of York 1974. Jeremy remembers this as an occasion when Nancy Richardson, Mary Guillemard and Stella Alexander appeared as staunch supporters.

Many members of FHF wanted to go further and have a broader kind of discussion and engagement with Friends generally. The Social Responsibility Council (SRC), which had taken the major step of publishing *Homosexuality from the inside* in 1973, eventually organised a conference with the theme 'Towards an understanding of sexual relationships' for April 1976. It was held at Hulme Hall, Manchester University, the same venue that was used for the gathering at which FHF was founded in September 1973. Monthly meetings were invited to send representatives, and the conference was attended by over 100 Friends. In a letter (24 April) to Roger Sawkins in Brisbane I wrote that it:

> went surprisingly well, considering the botched preparation that it suffered. About a hundred people came, about twenty-five gay. It was a very open conference, warm and accepting, but probably – despite the monthly meeting representation – a fairly self-selected group. In a way it was disappointing that not more people came who would take a rather traditional line on sexual questions, because I think we could not really regard ourselves as an adequate cross-section of Quaker opinion...There was no specific aim to the conference apart from mutual understanding, but several people felt a minute would be useful as a basis for Friends to report to their monthly meetings. However, once we embarked on this exercise, it was clear that a brief statement could not provide an accurate or adequate basis for unity, so the attempt was abandoned. I don't think this was a failure. We realised the difficulties of formulating statements about such complex matters.

Meanwhile, FHF embarked on a further piece of educational work among Friends. Information about FHF was sent in the spring of 1977 to all the local meetings within the area of London Yearly Meeting with a request to the clerk to bring it to the attention of the meeting. In his covering letter Michael Hutchinson, as Assistant Clerk of FHF, pointed out that the FHF existed 'in order to provide fellowship and support for homosexual and bisexual Friends and attenders and to promote wider understanding and acceptance within the Society.' In his conclusion he wrote: 'We would like to emphasise that we are a group within the Society that exists because of the needs of its members as Quakers.' What happened to this communication was very mixed. Some local meeting clerks were glad to receive the information and make it known, but others suppressed or neglected it, feeling, rightly or wrongly, that there was no one in the meeting to whom it would be relevant.

In August 1978 Yearly Meeting, held residentially for a week at Lancaster University, offered an opportunity for further consideration of gay issues. Some anxiety (or was it simply caution?) on the part of the Yearly Meeting officers was shown by the fact that the occasion was described in a curious way. It was not a session of Yearly Meeting in the usual sense, despite being clerked by the Yearly Meeting Clerk (Gillian E. Hopkins), but was arranged by the Agenda Committee and clerked by Roger C. Wilson[3]. It was scheduled for the Monday afternoon, and the speaker was Jeremy Greenwood, chosen by FHF. It was a partly personal, partly general talk rather than an introduction to a deliberation of Yearly Meeting leading to a minute. Special interest groups were arranged on the same evening with Irene Jacoby, Michael Hutchinson, Jeremy Greenwood and myself as facilitators. All went smoothly; there was no uproar. The talk was later printed in *The Friend*[4]. As there was no written reaction to it in *The Friend*, the South East Group of FHF arranged an afternoon at Westminster Meeting House on Saturday, 10 March 1979, details of which were circulated to all meetings within the area of London & Middlesex General Meeting.

It was nonetheless not all plain sailing in the years afterwards. Some Friends were clearly unhappy about the way in which things were going, but they were not very successful in putting their views across. Robin Hodgkin was one of these, and after *The Friend* published a short article of his on 'Friends and Relationships'[5] but declined further essays, he published a pamphlet of his own entitled *Created male and female*[6]. His unease went back as far as *Towards a Quaker view of sex*, but he was also doubtful about the suggestion made at Yearly Meeting 1981 that meetings might organise local discussion groups on what he called 'these vexed questions'. His pamphlet consisted of five short essays in which, basically, he reiterated the traditional Christian position, expressing the view that it was not too much for homosexuals to remain celibate. It is significant that his third essay was headed 'The achievement of heterosexuality'. While he wrote about sex as needing to be 'cherished and celebrated at the biological level and at many levels transcending biology,' his views were those of a married heterosexual man with no appreciation of what it meant emotionally and practically to be homosexual.

Meanwhile, FHF went on with its work. In October 1981 it published an eight-page pamphlet with articles by Monica Furlong entitled 'Shrinking and clinging' and Erica Vere called 'Transition to openness' and a postscript to *Homosexuality from the inside* by David Blamires. Its next initiative was much bigger and came to fruition in 1982. This was *Meeting gay Friends*, a collection of 22 autobiographical essays by members of FHF. It was edited by John Banks and Martina Weitsch and had an afterword by Mary Guillemard. The contributors were remarkably frank about themselves and their sexual struggles in both adolescence and adulthood; the age-range stretched from early twenties to pensionable age. There were fifteen men and eight women (two of the women, a couple, wrote a single contribution). Four men and one woman, for different reasons, decided to write anonymously. Two women and two men were either married or had been married; three of them also had children. The book as a whole amounted to 92 closely printed pages. One of the contributors wrote over eleven pages, two contented themselves with slightly over one, and there was everything else in between.

As I have re-read the pieces now (2010), nearly thirty years since they were first published, what most impresses me is how scrupulous the writers were about their sexual and emotional development, the ups and downs of their lives. They did not spare themselves or their future readers. One stated that it was the first time he'd written about his life as a homosexual in a heterosexual society. I suspect that for several of the contributors their writing was personally therapeutic and marked an important milestone in their lives. Their endeavour was really courageous. In the annals of gay writing this book is remarkable for the fact that, in an overwhelmingly secular society, it combines sexuality with spirituality in a truly authentic way. Each of the contributors speaks in his or her own voice, neither apologising nor proselytising. Their individuality comes across clearly, and so does their honesty. The book is, as one might expect, out of print, but it would be worth trying to track down a library or second-hand copy.

Although FHF was always principally focused on homosexuality, both male and female, it was clear from the start, as some of the pieces in *Meeting gay Friends* later made explicit, that bisexuality was part of the larger picture. At a later stage a couple of transgender Friends joined the group. It is worth noting that as early as the weekend conference of 25–29 April 1975, held at St Katharine's in London, Charlotte Wolff gave a talk on bisexuality. Charlotte Wolff had published in 1971 her book *Love between women* with Duckworth, and in 1977 Quartet published her *Bisexuality: a study*. She was introduced to us by Audrey Wood[7], who was a personal friend and neighbour[8]. During the period that I was active in FHF a small number of transsexual Friends joined the group, became a firm part of it and significantly broadened the understanding of the rest of us.

FHF conference topics ranged widely. We invited both fellow Quakers and people from other gay organisations to speak to us as well as using our own resources. On one occasion, at Hampstead FMH on 17 October 1978, Sarah Coggin of the Gay Christian Movement and Hugh Pyper, one of our own number, spoke to us on the theme of 'coming out' (still a relevant topic today). On the same occasion that Charlotte Wolff addressed us we also had Andrew Hodges of *Gay News* to speak on the booklet *With downcast gays: aspects of homosexual self-oppression*, which he and David Hutter had written[9]. It was a time when books and pamphlets proliferated with many different views being canvassed. Some of this was home grown, but a lot of it came from the United States. Gay Friends were a part of this ferment of ideas.

Links existed between individual gay Friends across the English-speaking world. Quakers in Britain were in touch with others in the United States, Canada, Australia and New Zealand and to a lesser extent with Friends in other parts of Europe. Where Friends in Ireland were concerned, it was usually the case that a few individuals needed to escape temporarily from the predominantly negative attitudes that were the norm in both Catholic and Protestant circles. Tom Bodine, a New England Friend who spent a lot of time in Britain after he retired, residing in Birmingham and full of energy and sociability, kept FHF constantly in touch with developments in the United States and among North American Quakers. His contribution to *Meeting gay Friends* illustrated the problems of being homosexual and moving between liberal Quaker organisations and the at times virulently anti-homosexual groupings that also exist in the US.

Tom believed in keeping channels of communication open between the different American yearly meetings and building bridges between opposing Quaker organisations. Matters almost came to breaking-point at the All American Friends Conference held at Wichita, Kansas, in the last week of July 1977. North America contains a great variety of types of Quakerism ranging from the liberal yearly meetings of East Coast America, worshipping on a basis of silence such as we practise in Britain, to the strongly Bible-based yearly meetings of the Mid West and the West Coast, which have programmed worship, pastors, sing hymns and are in many (but not all) ways like nonconformists. It was the desire of liberal Friends supporting the Friends Committee for Gay Concerns to be allowed to display literature that ignited opposition from the Evangelical wing. The Conference came near to collapse. However, long and patient discussion between the opposing groups, searching for ways in which they could unite without one side defeating the other, finally made it possible for the Conference to go ahead[10]. British Quakerism has not experienced this degree of confrontation, though it certainly has been challenged over the issue of homosexuality on a variety of occasions, as we have already seen and will see more of in this historical account.

FHF continued its campaigning work among British Quakers alongside enjoying regular gatherings for mutual support, discussion, conviviality and worship. From the period of its early existence there had been a number of local or regional groups as well as nationally organised activities. These flourished mainly in the densely populated South-East of England, but there were other groups active from time to time in East Anglia, the Bristol and Oxford areas, the Midlands, the North of England and Scotland. Distance and difficulties of transport often threatened the viability of the smaller groups, so the pattern was one of change rather than constancy. Similarly, as new members joined and old ones left, those able and willing to maintain the national organisation changed too. Over the whole period, however, FHF has demonstrated its continuing existence through regular advertisements in *The Friend* and the gay press.

Eleven years after the publication of *Meeting gay Friends* another booklet of a quite different kind was published by the group. By this time, following the spirit of the age, FHF had changed its name to Quaker Lesbian and Gay Fellowship (QLGF). 'Quaker' was a clearer, less ambiguous name than 'Friends', and 'Lesbian and Gay' showed that the group included both women and men. The term 'homosexual' had virtually disappeared from gay usage. *Speaking our truth: a plain Quaker's guide to lesbian and gay lives* was a short, accessible booklet attempting to answer the commonest questions in the space of 24 pages[11]. And as Alice thought, 'What use is a book without pictures?' it contained four cartoon-type illustrations by John Rowe. Given the frequent changes in the laws affecting lesbian and gay people over the period from 1967 to the present day, publications did not have a long shelf-life before they became significantly out of date. *Speaking our truth* was thus revised in 2004 and given a new title – *Part of the rainbow: a plain Quaker look at lesbian gay and bisexual lives*. The booklet was further updated in 2008 and expanded to 38 pages of text.

As I only learnt about *Speaking our truth* and *Part of the rainbow* (in its two versions) after they were published, I can only express my admiration for their tone and clarity. Information is provided about a range of likely questions from people with doubts or uncertainties, correcting popular misconceptions. The whole booklet is deeply grounded in Quaker thought and practice, beginning with *Advices & queries 22*:

Respect the whole diversity among us in our lives and relationships. Refrain from making prejudiced judgements about the life journeys of others. Do you foster the spirit of mutual understanding and forgiveness which our discipleship asks of us? Remember that each one of us is unique, precious, a child of God.

Part of the rainbow includes a number of telling examples of individual experience, both positive and negative, which complement the common-sense generalities of the rest of the pamphlet. As was the case with *Towards a Quaker view of sex* and *Homosexuality from the inside*, the booklet concludes with a list of useful addresses and helpful books.

FHF and QLGF issued regular newsletters from the early 1970s onwards. At first these were intended only for members of the Fellowship because of the nature of the times, but later they were distributed without such restrictions. Friends House Library maintains a complete set. The newsletters provide details of conferences, talks, book reviews, correspondence and so on. Many Quaker meetings subscribed to them. They formed an important link between gay Friends and the rest of British Quakers. Details about FHF/QLGF were also given in the list of unofficial Quaker bodies printed in the annual *Book of Meetings* and the Yearly Meeting *Documents in advance*. QLGF is still alive and its involvement with later issues and events in our story will surface in other chapters.

4

Towards recognition

By the beginning of the 1980s all kinds of questions about homosexuality were surfacing in society at large. At issue were matters to do with social and legal equality of treatment between homosexuals and heterosexuals. These had been present earlier, but now Quakers were being challenged to consider them as they affected Quaker values and practices. The most tricky of these questions focused on what, for brevity's sake, we may call 'gay marriage'. In the first instance, it was concerned with the recognition of same-sex relationships. Should Friends offer gay couples the same care and support as heterosexual couples received in marriage? If so (and it was not a foregone conclusion), what should this be called? Would it be 'marriage', 'union', 'celebration of commitment' or something else? British Quakers did not find it easy or straightforward to make clear decisions.

Susan Hartshorne, a heterosexual married woman and lawyer belonging to Mount Street Meeting, Manchester, was particularly concerned about the question of equality between gay and straight couples. As a magistrate she had put a proposal to the Manchester Bench that the age of consent should be the same for both gay and straight individuals, namely sixteen, and it was unanimously agreed on 17 March 1986. Susan brought her concern about equality between gay and straight couples in regard to religious marriage to Manchester Preparative Meeting on Sunday, 9 November 1986. It was supported and sent on to Hardshaw East Monthly Meeting (now renamed as Manchester and Warrington Area Meeting), which appointed a special monthly meeting on Sunday afternoon, 22 March 1987, at Eccles to consider it. I wrote a detailed account of this meeting in my diary, from which I quote below. Many of the points made on that occasion typically cropped up in Quaker discussions elsewhere. I have divided my diary text into paragraphs, replaced some names by initials and made one or two minor omissions. This is what I noted as significant:

> Several of us took sandwiches to Eccles for lunch, as at 2.30 there was the special MM convened to consider Susan Hartshorne's concern about the lack of provision for same-sex marriages among Friends. It was quite the most remarkable MM I've been to. For one thing the turn-out was phenomenal. Our usual attendance is 25–30, but there must have been 70 present & that without any representation from Warrington or Westhoughton. Lawrence Martins felt the need for an additional asst. clerk, pref. a woman, so Janet Quilley was appointed to join him and Chris Lukey at the table. Chris had read in the mtg for worship that section of the <u>Advices</u> (IV, para. 2) that says 'Think it possible that you may be mistaken'. Minutes from gps of Fds at Oldham, Warrington & (?) Eccles spoke positively about the concern, but didn't like the use of the word 'marriage'. Susan then gave a v. well prepared introduction – really excellently done.
>
> The contributions that followed, whatever the shade of opinion, were all expressed calmly & in a worshipful manner. There was a fair amount of worry abt the word 'marriage', & a few Fds were clearly disturbed about

homosexuality generally, though Lawrence made it clear
we were not there to discuss that. As an issue that already
seemed to have been accepted by Fds, he implied. WB,
standing right behind me, cd not accept Susan's proposal
because it wasn't scriptural. JG said we all knew what
'marriage' meant & that it cdn't be applied to homosexual
relationships. She was afraid of how the media wd deal
with the proposal & that adverse publicity wd damage Fds
work.

But actually the gt majority of contributions were extremely
supportive – John Sheldon said he felt he'd been listening
to truth when Susan was speaking. Clare Whitehead said
her own experience of marriage had led her to believe
that any similar experience betw. gay people was a cause
for celebration. She spoke very simply & movingly & was
close to tears. Indeed much of the tenor of contributions
generally was like that of deeply felt ministry in mtg for
worship.

William Wood said he'd come with an open mind to the
mtg, & he now felt we shd not avoid the use of the word
'marriage', that it was the right word. Pat Lee spoke abt
valuing the contributions of gay Fds to the life of the
Society, referring almost explicitly to me [...]. GL also
had a contribution to make & it was not to express her
opposition on scriptural grounds, but it was rather on the
grounds that what God blesses by way of personal calling
(being single in her case) or personal relationships doesn't
need to be formalised in a ritual. MS spoke movingly abt
the 10 yrs of heterosexual marriage ended amicably &
her new life with J. John Banks said he didn't want Fds'
sympathy, but rather being accepted as a fellow human
being. It's difficult to give more than a smattering of the
kinds of things said, but it was altogether a quite amazing

& unique occasion. Abt ten or a dozen attenders had
requested permission to be present...

We broke for a cup of tea round 4.30, while the clerks
struggled to formulate a minute. That took ¾ hr. Lawrence
gave overmuch weight to the 'opposition', I feel, but while
we were not united on one recommendation, we were
clear enough that there was a subject to which Mtg for
Sufferings shd give its attention. It was only at this point
of forwarding the minute to Sufferings that I made any
vocal contribution to the discussion, simply hoping that
this was what we wd do.

Susan Hartshorne spoke to this minute at Meeting for Sufferings
on 4 July 1987. In its minute Sufferings said among other things:
'We can expect that some committed homosexual couples will
ask their meetings for a celebration of their commitment to each
other. Meetings already have the means whereby meetings for
worship can be held for this purpose.' The full minute later was
included in *Quaker faith & practice*[1], and was also printed in *The
Friend*[2]. Sufferings asked its Nominations Committee 'to bring in
the name of a small group of Friends present in this meeting to
prepare a suitable document.' The Friends appointed to this Same-
sex Relationship Group were Kathleen Cottrell, Ann Cuming (an
early heterosexual member of FHF), Jo Farrow (General Secretary
of Quaker Home Service), Susan Hartshorne and Michael
Hutchinson (also a member of FHF). They reported to Sufferings
on 7 May 1988, having prepared a paper on 'The recognition of
same-sex relationships in our meetings' along with a summary of
the discussion on 4 July 1987. They also brought an outline of their
proposed study pack. Sufferings was not able to endorse the report,
and its minute stated: 'This matter is an extremely difficult one
for many of us.' It appointed Harold Chamings to join the group
and asked the Yearly Meeting Agenda Committee "to consider

whether this matter could find some place in 1989 YM"[3]. It ended by thanking the group for its continuing work.

The response of Sufferings reflected the uncertainty and reluctance of the times, but it resulted in a fine comprehensive study pack dated October 1988, compiled by the Same-sex Relationship Group and distributed by Quaker Home Service. It was entitled *The recognition of same-sex relationships in the Religious Society of Friends* and consisted of 46 pages of documents produced by a variety of Quaker bodies and some other Christian organisations. As well as reproducing relevant minutes it includes sections on:

- the meaning of love in the New Testament;
- the nurturing of relationships;
- the Quaker marriage tradition;
- sexuality;
- homosexuality and the Bible;
- homosexuality and same-sex relationships in some USA yearly meetings;
- relationships other than marriage in Australia Yearly Meeting;
- clearness meetings;
- advising same-sex couples: the legal position;
- statements by some churches on homosexuality;
- a Mothers' Union pamphlet;
- a reading list.

It is an extraordinarily valuable collection of material that would be difficult to track down anywhere else. It is not clear to what extent it was used by meetings and individuals since it was little publicised or promoted, but it was an important aid in the development of Quaker thinking. Susan Hartshorne was ahead of her time in her concern for equal recognition of same-sex relationships, which did not return to Yearly Meeting until 2009.

Susan's concern was an individual one that was tested in a monthly meeting and then forwarded to Meeting for Sufferings, where effectively it was shelved, though the small committee appointed by Sufferings prepared helpful and challenging study material. Susan's concern was not an abstract one, but arose from her personal reaction to a gay friend of hers who had, easily and naturally, used the word "marry" to describe his 16-year-long relationship with his partner. She could not see the quality of their relationship as being different from her own marriage. What is more, they would have liked the opportunity of some kind of religious ceremony to mark their commitment and love.

In 1988 British Quakers had the opportunity of a more sharply focused encounter with gay experience. At Yearly Meeting the Swarthmore Lecture was given by Harvey Gillman with the intriguing title of *A minority of one*. It was a powerful, electrifying presentation with crescendos and quiet passages, anger and harmony, prose and poetry. It attracted lots of positive reactions at the end. Harvey had first of all worked at Friends House as Publications Secretary for Quaker Peace & Service, but left QPS in 1983 to become Extension (later renamed Outreach) Secretary of Quaker Home Service. He was (and is) well known among British Friends as a thoughtful and challenging speaker on the nature of the spiritual life. In his Swarthmore Lecture he explored three fundamentals of his life – his Jewish background, the gradual growth of his awareness of being gay, and his discovery of Quakerism. There is a continuing interplay between these three elements, but all of them relate to the experience of belonging to a disempowered minority.

What was refreshing and different about Harvey's presentation was its positive viewpoint. Was this perhaps the first time that most of his audience and readers heard of "*the gift* of being gay", which is how the section dealing with gayness is called? It occupies a mere 15 pages of the whole book, but packs its punches. It deals with the problems of growing up gay and lacking positive role models, but Harvey goes on to write about what the gifts of being gay are for himself. "The first somewhat ambiguous gift," he says, "lies in the fact that I have not been able to accept ready-made value systems. I have been forced to create my values out of my search for personal truth and to recognise that my awareness of these values has changed as my experience has deepened"[4]. That is a statement with which gay people will readily agree, though it also applies to many Quakers who are not gay.

Harvey's second gift centres on contemporary attitudes towards masculinity. "Being gay has enabled me to try to reach beyond the dualistic polarisation of masculinity/femininity. My observations have led me to note that commonly accepted masculine and feminine norms can be destructive to all people"[5]. This is of course not a new idea, but it is important to reiterate it. Many men in our society, having been brought up to be brave and not cry, find it difficult to express tenderness, especially towards other men.

The third gift is linked with this. It is "the perception that just as we can see that masculinity and femininity are not opposites but are mutually redeeming, so we have the vision that all creation is a unity and that each one of us is a microcosm of the whole"[6]. Harvey admits that one doesn't have to be gay to reach this conclusion, he is simply describing how it was for himself.

He sympathises with gay people who are hostile towards the media and the churches, but he goes on to say that the Quaker Peace Testimony is important to him

> not because it comes easily, but precisely because I find it so terribly difficult to put into practice. Anger and resentment are two emotions I have still to come to terms with. And yet at the same time there is a great joy in being alive and in the fact that so many have refused to be browbeaten in spite of the pressure upon them to conform to what are for them false ways of living[7].

During the 1980s British Quakers were thus confronted with a concern that arose through an individual Friend and also, in the Swarthmore Lecture, by the very public expression of experience by a gay man who worked with Quaker Home Service and was well known throughout the Society. Susan Hartshorne's concern was a challenge that Meeting for Sufferings was not ready wholeheartedly to meet, and its response was a disappointment to many Friends. But with Harvey Gillman the Society was ready to acknowledge publicly the contribution of a gay man to the life and work of the whole body of Friends. Friends House of course recognised and valued the work of many other "out" gay people who worked nationally for the Society, and in a sense Harvey was their public voice. The Swarthmore Lecture Committee is not part of the Yearly Meeting structure, but is appointed by Woodbrooke. However, the fact that the Lecture is traditionally given on the occasion that the Yearly Meeting is held means that unofficially it addresses and is recognised by the national body.

We can, I think, see Susan's concern and Harvey's lecture as pointing *towards recognition* of gay rights and gay experience, but the 1980s were also a decade in which other powers and movements reversed the progress towards equality. It is to this that I now turn.

5

HIV/AIDS and 'Clause 28'

If ever an acronym conveyed a meaning diametrically opposed to what it suggests, AIDS is the one. It does not suggest help or assistance being at hand, but rather disaster. The initials stand for Acquired Immune Deficiency Syndrome, and it represents the most extreme development of the chronic viral infection HIV or the Human Immunodeficiency Virus. A person infected with HIV is known as HIV positive – another appellation that suggests the opposite of what it appears to say, since *positive* usually means good, while negative is bad. The terminology for this infection perhaps reflects the confusion and horror that surrounds it even today, thirty years on from the first description of it was made in the United States in 1981.

AIDS was first recognised in the Western world and was overwhelmingly identified with gay men, as a result of which it was typecast as a gay disease. Now it is known throughout the world and is no respecter of sexual orientation or of sexual maturity. The majority of people carrying the virus live and die in Africa, where its effect on populations is catastrophic; they are largely heterosexual.

It is not the purpose of this chapter to give a detailed account of HIV/AIDS from the medical angle. When it first appeared it was incurable and led sooner or later, and often distressingly, to death. It is now, thirty years later, better understood, and great advances have been made in treatment, though the relevant drugs are not readily available to all those who would benefit from them. The poor, as always, lose out. Nor is it possible here to deal with the political, religious and social obstacles that have been put in the way of effective medical treatment. The history of AIDS is both complex and disturbing.

Most gay people in Britain will have known or know friends, acquaintances or relatives with AIDS. One of the friends who had lived in my house in the late 1970s died suddenly of AIDS in the autumn of 1985 aged 34. I hadn't known of the seriousness of his illness, nor had his parents. In 1988 I learnt that a vibrant, sociable Quaker friend of mine in Canada had died and that an academic friend was HIV+. Two colleagues and friends at the University died. A Young Friend in Manchester also succumbed to the disease. I mention them because they had particular significance for me as I knew them personally, but many other Quakers could tell similar stories. A huge number of biographical, autobiographical and fictionalised accounts have been published in books, magazines, plays and films, each telling a story that is both the same and yet different because human beings are all different.

People who had AIDS were frequently ostracised or victimised rather than sympathised with. Since male homosexuality, despite the partial decriminalisation of 1967, was still regarded by many people as wicked or sinful, AIDS was commonly regarded as a just punishment for illicit sexual intercourse. People who had caught the virus, but not through sexual intercourse, were described as innocent sufferers. AIDS was also regarded – wrongly – as a contagious, not as an infectious disease, and this created tremendous fear and anxiety about touching, using or coming into contact with items that belonged to an AIDS sufferer.

During 1987 I had been invited by the trustees of *The Friend*

Publications to take on the editorship of the *Friends Quarterly*. It so happened that 1988 was the twenty-fifth anniversary of the publication of *Towards a Quaker view of sex*, so I was urged to take this as an opportunity to put together in the October 1988 issue a set of articles on 'Friends and sexuality'. These covered a broad range of topics; they were not restricted to homosexuality. Among them was an article by Gordon Macphail[1] entitled 'A Quaker doctor's experience of AIDS', which provided sober information and attempted to answer a variety of frequent questions. Gordon lived in Brighton and had wide experience of gay patients, among them some with AIDS, whom he cared for not only medically, but also from the pastoral point of view.

After giving factual information about the disease as then known, Gordon went on to ask searching questions such as "What is it like to have AIDS?" and "What is it like to be antibody positive?" Among the greatest problems were the reactions of other people, relatives, friends and acquaintances, religious people. Gordon's first patient with AIDS was accepted by some Anglican nuns for a period of respite care. He wrote: "Brian nearly refused this offer. It was not long after a Police Chief and professed Christian had claimed to be God's prophet and said that homosexuals were 'swirling in a cesspit of their own making'. If this was Christian love, what could you expect from nuns?" Gordon also expressed his own feelings: "I often felt useless and inadequate. I found it difficult to go there and be with such pain, and yet I know that just being there is often more important than anything you can do. I was greatly enriched by the way it taught me to be more loving."

In his article Gordon mentioned a conference on AIDS and Pastoral Care that Quaker Social Responsibility and Education (QSRE) and Woodbrooke, the Quaker college in Selly Oak, Birmingham, organised together in April 1988. It was one of the occasions when more than individual responses to the AIDS crisis were evoked. An open meeting of elders and overseers was held at the conference and produced the following minute:

> We have met together prayerfully to consider the AIDS crisis. This has been a painful experience for us. We have examined our prejudices in the face of the God-given diversity of human sexuality. As we have done this we have grown closer and more understanding of one another.
> The experience of AIDS can be one of suffering in fearful isolation; but it can also be a challenge to us as Quakers to translate our faith into practical action, and to let our lives speak of that accepting love which casts out fear.
> Some of us feel a Call to travel in the Ministry to share with other Friends what we have been given and have given to one another. We recommend that QSRE set up a working party to look for ways of taking [the Concern on AIDS] forward. However, there is a Concern laid upon all of us to promote urgent discussion throughout the whole of this Yearly Meeting of the issues raised by AIDS.

Discussion of AIDS necessitated first a discussion of attitudes towards homosexuality, so even in this critical situation of pain and distress there was some unexpected progress towards a better understanding. Gordon concluded his article by declaring: "It is the central Christian experience that the power of love can transform suffering and death into an opportunity for life and light and new growth. Many of those involved with AIDS have found this in their own lives, though perhaps few would use these Christian terms to describe their experiences. Is the Society of Friends ready for God's challenge?"

Gordon wrote another article taking matters further. Entitled 'AIDS, sin and the Society of Friends'[2], it focuses directly and acutely on the pastoral and personal questions that AIDS faces us with. Some Friends will be made very uncomfortable:

By no means all people with AIDS are ill-used saints, but it is among people with AIDS that I have met the healing power of divine love. I did not expect to meet this Living Christ, but where else would he be but dining with social outcasts? Perhaps what I have to write about is not what the Society of Friends has to say to people with AIDS, but what people with AIDS have to offer the Society of Friends. There is hope for us yet: much contemporary Quaker writing is about our need for spiritual renewal. AIDS is coming to affect us all – God's challenge to Quakers. The body of the Society of Friends already has AIDS. If approached in accepting love, it can sometimes bring us to healing of the spirit.

Gordon did not write directly of his own HIV infection in either of these two articles, since he was not concerned with self but with broader issues to do with the nature of Christian community. He died in 1991 a few days after his 35th birthday. Chichester Monthly Meeting wrote a long testimony to the grace of God as shown in his life. It ends tellingly with a quotation from the Apocrypha[3]: "There is nothing so precious as a faithful friend, and no scales can measure his excellence. A faithful friend is a medicine of life; and those who fear the Lord will find him."

I do not know how much local Quaker involvement there was on AIDS issues within the compass of London Yearly Meeting. Probably individuals did what they could in their own locality. A small group of Manchester Friends met on 24 August 1989 to see what we could or should do as a meeting to help. An ecumenical consultation took place at Bishopscourt, the residence of the Bishop of Manchester, on 7 October, at which Quakers were the most strongly represented group. Among the others was a representative from the AIDS Time for Support group, which was involved with practical work. The consultation resulted in the establishment of a small ecumenical prayer group that was supported by Canon Alan Gawith of the Church of England Board of Social Responsibility, whom I knew from previous C of E discussions of homosexuality following the Anglican report on *Homosexual relationships* (1979). The prayer group met at an Anglican church near my home. It was only ever a very small group with four to ten people attending and did not continue for very long, but it was worthwhile nonetheless. Other towns and cities probably had similar activities that concerned Quakers participated in, as it was particularly in large urban areas that people with AIDS were likely to be found. Edinburgh Friends, for example, set up an advisory service in the late 1980s, and in 1990 Frank Boulton got involved in local public health initiatives on behalf of Southampton Meeting. Quaker Social Responsibility and Education held a second conference at Woodbrooke in 1991, but as time progressed it became clear that there was no need for continuing official Quaker involvement. A number of individual Quakers with particular specialist input did of course continue to work in this area.

AIDS posed a nasty problem to Christians (among them Quakers too). Some, sticking to austere principles, remained apart, while others accepted the challenge of showing love and respect to all who were suffering. It has been the mark of many Christian communities and countries that they have been slow to offer help when it was needed. The greatest help has come from other gay people.

But AIDS was not the only problem confronting gays in Britain in the late 1980s. Despite the fact that the law had been changed twenty years earlier in England and Wales, there were people around who would have liked to turn the clock back drastically. 1988 was the year of 'Clause 28' and eventually 'Section 28' of the Local Government Act 1988, brought in by the Conservative Government headed by Margaret Thatcher. It sought to restrict severely the ways in which gay people could act and present themselves and it did this by attacking the activities of local authorities, as follows:

(1) A local authority shall not –
    (a) intentionally promote homosexuality or publish material with the intent of promoting homosexuality;
    (b) promote the teaching in any maintained school of the acceptability of homosexuality as a pretended family relationship.
(2) Nothing in subsection (1) above shall be taken to prohibit the doing of anything for the purpose of treating or preventing the spread of disease.
(3) In any proceedings in connection with the application of this section a court shall draw such inferences as to the intention of the local authority as may reasonably be drawn from the evidence before it.

The oddities, the broad, undefined concepts, deficiencies and implications of this formulation were discussed in detail by Tina Day, a member of FHF, in an article entitled 'Clause 28: Pushing the Invisible back from the Light' in the *Friends Quarterly*[4]. As far as I am aware, there were no prosecutions of a local authority as a result of Section 28, but its aims were achieved through the self-censorship of authorities who did not want to be entangled in complex legal arguments. They were cautious and did not test the limits of what was permissible. The complaint of just one parent, if upheld, could prove ruinous.

It is not appropriate in this context to discuss Clause 28 and its implications in detail, but it did make a mark among Quakers in various parts of the country. As one might expect, FHF held a special interest group devoted to the subject at Yearly Meeting (31 May 1988), just a week after Section 28 had come into effect (24 May). There had been a demonstration in London on 9 January, before

Clause 28 had been voted on, and several Quakers joined this. On 20 February there was a march in Manchester. This happened to be the day that Lancashire & Cheshire General Meeting was held at Mount Street, and several Mount Street Friends absented themselves from the meeting in order to join the demonstration for Lesbian and Gay Rights against Clause 28. I noted in my diary:

> The Marxist political gps were v. prominent with their banners & Socialist workers, & it was difficult to avoid being seen as part of their visible presence. The police adopted a v. low profile & were v. few in number Their estimate of numbers, retailed on the 6 o'clock BBC4 news, was 15,000, so probably there were quite a few more. It was certainly Manchester's biggest march for a long time. I wd guess 95% of the participants were in their 20s. Not many v. noticeable heterosexuals, but then if they were like John W. or Trevor, by themselves, they wdn't have stood out as straight. A certain amount of noisy, aggressive chanting of slogans that wd have been no help in attracting others to the cause, but otherwise basically good-tempered. I didn't see any antagonism from the crowds in the city centre who saw us passing... I wish I'd seen more people I knew, but perhaps they were elsewhere in the crowd.

Interestingly, at a meeting for worship that was packed with General Meeting teenagers the day after, Trevor Allcock spoke about the march and the fact that fifty years ago to the day the Nazis passed the same kind of law.

I hesitate to comment on these demonstrations from the vantage point of more than thirty years later. I'm not the kind of person that does it easily. Quakers on the whole like to be in charge or in the forefront of worthy causes, particularly if there is a peace element to it. Although several straight Friends showed their solidarity and joined in the Manchester march, there would have been many more if it had been a peace rally. The Government was perhaps taken aback at the strength of opposition to Clause 28, but the Bill was passed anyway. Quakers as a corporate body had almost nothing to say about it.

6

This we can say, and what Yearly Meeting said in 1994/95

Towards a Quaker view of sex, first published in 1963 and revised in 1964, had been a Quaker bestseller, but by 1987 it had become completely outdated. Whatever conservative congregations in other parts of the world still had to tackle, changes in social attitudes towards various aspects of sexual conduct were enormous, and of course changes in the law had made homosexuality more acceptable. It seemed to the Literature Committee of Quaker Home Service that a new Quaker look at sex would be a good thing. Could a new approach perhaps update or replace *Towards a Quaker view of sex*?

Like the group that wrote *TQVS*, we (the group that took on the task) were not nominated and appointed by an official Quaker body, but had support from QHS to finance our meetings. The group consisted of five men and five women: David Blamires, Loraine Brown, June Ellis, Colin Hunter, Christine Knott, Gordon Macphail, Neil Pickering, Elisabeth Salisbury, Chris Skidmore and Zoe White. Elisabeth, June, Christine, Colin and myself knew each other through QHS Representative Council and various committees. June was one of the co-wardens of Woodbrooke.

Loraine had written an article on 'What marriage looks like in the 1980s' for the *Friends Quarterly*[1], and Gordon had written likewise about AIDS. I'm not sure how Chris and Zoe came to be part of the group, but Neil came in as a Young Friend.

One thing differentiated us clearly from the group, and that was that we were not chosen for our professional qualifications. Six members of the group were married, four of us were single. Our ages ran from the late twenties to about sixty. The group included a variety of lifestyles: bisexual, gay, heterosexual, lesbian, some living with partners, others alone. One person was divorced and another was separated from a partner. But it was only as we started talking about ourselves in more detail that we realised how varied our life experiences were.

We quickly realised that we could not, and did not want to, produce a Quaker guide to sexual ethics. We were not in the business of prescribing how people should live their lives, but it was implicit in our thinking that sex lays on us responsibilities and choices as well as joy and pain. These encompass our partners, friends and other members of our family as well as wider social groupings. We were not concerned with sexual orientation as such, but an awareness of the differences between gay, lesbian and straight experience was often on our minds.

I have found it quite difficult, looking at *This we can say* from the perspective of fifteen years later, to know what I can say. As a group we produced a considerable quantity of written material from which we selected rigorously to form the actual book. Each of the papers or documents was written by a particular individual, but we decided not to identify individuals, as we wanted the whole book to be taken as what we stood by. In a sense it is not important who wrote which piece, though in a few cases it may be obvious. In many instances what is said is private and personal and has to remain anonymous.

The group first met on Sunday afternoon, 3 July 1988, at the

Quaker International Centre, Byng Place, London, and that was the venue for most of our subsequent meetings. At this first meeting we did not all know each other, so the main part of our time was taken up by introducing ourselves. It was risky. What should each of us say with regard to the subject that had brought us together? At least one person was daunted by the prospect and was not sure about staying as part of the group. This initial go-round was crucial for our process. We worked according to the pattern of creative listening, that is, each person spoke in turn and was listened to by the rest without any questioning or interruption. It was permissible to ask a brief clarificatory question, but nothing critical. Only when all the persons present had had their go would further contributions or general discussion be allowed. The point was that each person should feel safe, particularly if they had painful or delicate matters to share. With a group of this kind it was essential to observe confidentiality.

At this first meeting we decided to meet on a regular basis at roughly six-weekly intervals; sometimes it was less, sometimes more. Between 3 July 1988 and 11 December 1994 we met on a total of thirty-nine occasions, usually for three or four hours on a Sunday afternoon. We had four weekend meetings, of which three took place at The Gilletts at Charney Manor, where we worked intensively on the format of the final book. The whole process was demanding, especially for those members of the group who had far to travel (Brussels, Herefordshire, Ilkley, Manchester; Weymouth, later Plymouth). We did our best to meet immediately after Quaker business meetings in London that some members were committed to. Of course, not all the ten of us could manage every meeting.

After 10 December 1989 Gordon Macphail was too ill to continue with our regular meetings, though Christine Knott brought him for a last heroic attendance on 21 July 1991. Loraine Brown went into hospital for serious surgery in New Year 1991 and thereafter was unable to attend any of our meetings, though she did send us papers she had written. These were emotionally draining experiences for the group as a whole, but the ongoing commitment to be honest was an equal pressure. It would be untrue to claim that we worked harmoniously together all the time. Each of us had demands on time and energy from our ordinary lives as well as testing moments from other members of the group. Despite the pressures I think that each one of us would regard our experience of working together as a high point in our Quaker lives.

The papers that we wrote for each other bear a generic similarity to the kind of thing that was published in *Meeting gay Friends* and to parts of Harvey Gillman's Swarthmore Lecture. The talking parts of our meetings, in which we focused on a particular theme, in some ways resembled consciousness-raising activities, women's groups and men's groups that were common at the time. We decided on themes in advance so that we had time to ruminate on what we would say, but the result was more spontaneous than carefully prepared. The topics that we considered were extremely diverse: spirituality and sexuality, shame and guilt, parents and children, money, passion and eroticism, failure, jealousy and possessiveness, the difficulty of talking about personal sexual experience, marriage, sexual boundaries, love and loss, griefs and pain, relationships with parents, variety in sexual experience, cultural relativity, disgust, pornography, fantasy, sado-masochism, being a man and being a woman.

This was a wide-ranging set of topics, and most of us could contribute something to them. It was possible for anybody, however, to remain silent. Some of the topics proved hard to deal with on account of individual lack of experience. Others were difficult because of deep personal involvement. I am sure there were times when most, if not all, of us held back through anxiety about how we would be heard. We were, after all, tackling topics that many Friends were unwilling to face themselves.

From the wide range of the papers we produced we chose

excerpts for the book and grouped them according to the following headings: Our Quaker tradition and its consequences; The group's process; Living fully; Becoming ourselves; Confronting our uncertainties; Celebrating our sexuality; Suffering and failing; Emerging into wholeness; Together in friendship. Our hope was that the book would help Friends to develop their thinking on sex and sexuality, and to this end we appended eleven queries to assist personal responses and group discussion. When we had our material arranged to our own satisfaction, we sent copies in to four independent readers: Beth Allen, Ben Pink Dandelion, Susan Hartshorne and Christopher Holdsworth. When we received their reports we were discomfited to find that each of them had reservations about what we had metaphorically shed tears and blood over. We did not feel that we could materially change what we had done. The Literature Committee of QHS did not feel able to recommend publication. This left us with the option of having to publish the text ourselves. The result was *This we can say: Talking honestly about sex*[2], published by Nine Friends Press. It had to be Nine to be true to the fact that Gordon had died, but he is an integral part of the book.

As I reflect now (2010) on the book, I am less surprised that QHS Literature Committee did not accept *This we can say* as something that Quaker Home Service should publish. Our book did not come out strongly either for or against some of the thorny issues of the times, for example abortion, pornography, feeling that society's views were artificially polarised. Our position was more like that of Jesus refusing to make clear-cut judgements – "Let him who is without guilt cast the first stone."

We were over-optimistic in imagining that Friends in local meetings would be ready to explore pointed questions about sex and sexuality. It is easier to talk about personal sexual experience to strangers or to people you are not likely to meet on a frequent, friendly basis. Counsellors are very aware of this and build their practice around this. Sexual behaviour in our society is essentially private; it's not part of the conversational gambits of the middle class, though people readily comment on a public figure's being caught in the glare of media exposure,

We received an extremely encouraging review in the *Australian Friend* by Charles Stevenson, the editor, who wrote as follows:

> Every once in a while a book leaps out of its pages. 'This We Can Say' is one such book. Perhaps it is because of its integrity. Perhaps it is the boldness, yet humility, of their understanding of Quakerism – 'Our faith does not provide us with any kind of feather-bedding,' they say. Perhaps it strikes a deep chord within the heart of the reader.
>
> This book is something very beautiful, magnificent in places, and moving. One finds oneself wanting to learn by heart so many of their pithy statements. 'Absolute, unalterable rules do not take account of the sheer untidiness of life.' And 'Spirituality, like sexuality, is about darkness as well as light.' ...
>
> The book is a result of a group of Friends of various ages and sexual orientations coming together over a long period to consider rewriting *Towards a Quaker View of Sex*. They have not produced any definitive Quaker statement of sexuality, indeed their book is an independent publication. They...now share what they have found, not in a mighty proclamation, but from their own experience. They wish to celebrate the gift of sexuality, but know that when we fail there can be rejection and damage: 'Suffering, conflict, misjudgement, betrayal are recognised as part of being human.'

Our work on *This we can say* coincided temporally with the work of the Revision Committee appointed by Yearly Meeting to revise its Book of Discipline agreed in 1959 and first printed in 1960. Over the period from September 1986 to August 1994 the Committee's twenty-five members worked on a much larger project than ours, but it included one chapter, entitled 'Close Relationships', which covered similar ground. This became chapter 22 in our present *Quaker faith & practice*[3]. Past revisions of the Book of Discipline normally contented themselves with bringing the book up to date, dropping outdated material and adding new passages from Yearly Meeting and other minutes as well as extracts from the writings of Friends. This time the Revision Committee sought suggestions from individuals, who provided over 3,200 extracts, letters and minutes, which the Committee went through extremely carefully. The 1995 *Quaker faith & practice*, from its title downwards (*Quaker*, not *Christian*), is the most thoroughly revised Book of Discipline we have ever had and provides a comprehensive picture of British Friends today.

Two special Yearly Meetings were held in the spring and summer of 1994 to consider the text. I am concerned here only with the chapter on 'Close Relationships', which was taken in the summer meeting. Its eighty-one sections were arranged under the headings 'Friendship', 'Sexuality', 'Sharing a Home or Living Alone' (of which 'The single life' was a subsection), 'Marriage and Steadfast Commitment' with a subsection on 'Facing change and difficulty', 'Parents and Children', 'Ending of Relationships' and 'Bereavement'. Interestingly, there is no heading for 'Homosexuality', and the index to the 1995 agreed text directs the reader looking for 'homosexuality' to 'sexuality'. In this way the Revision Committee made the point that homosexuality was not to be considered as a separate topic or as inherently a problem. The tenor of the chapter as a whole was pastoral rather than dogmatic or theoretical; there was no specific engagement with interpretation of the Bible in regard to questions such as adultery, divorce or male homosexuality.

Before looking at how Yearly Meeting dealt with the matter it is instructive to look at some general points. *Christian faith and practice* (1959/60) concentrated its attention on 'Marriage and the Home'[4], adding a mere couple of paragraphs entitled 'Sexual morality'[5] sandwiched between 'Betting and gambling' and 'Administration of justice' in the chapter devoted to 'Social responsibilities'. There seems to have been at that time the tacit supposition that the problems lay outside the Society of Friends and that Friends differed little from other Christian churches with regard to sex. The previous revision (1922), with a division into two volumes – *Christian life faith and thought* and *Church government* – had no comment on sex at all.

Between 1960 and 1994 attitudes towards sex and sexuality changed enormously in society at large. Methods of artificial contraception, especially 'the pill', became widely available, pre-marital sex became more common, the law dealing with male homosexuality was changed in 1967, and attitudes towards teenage pregnancies and unmarried mothers softened. Quakers were not unaffected by these changes. The Religious Society of Friends is not a self-contained body going its own careful (or often challenging) way. But the changes among Friends did not happen all at once; they were gradual and piecemeal.

Previous editions of the Book of Discipline, as mentioned above, tended to consist of Yearly Meeting minutes and extracts from the writings of weighty Friends. It was unusual to have purely personal statements. This was perhaps the biggest change made by the 1994 revision. Certainly as far as 'Close relationships' was concerned, there was a move away from tested corporate positions to a range of possibilities of belief and sincere conduct. Some of these passages appeared anonymously, while others were credited to a particular individual. The 1994 Draft gave forty-six post-1950 personal statements, and this increased in the printed book to fifty-four, which was rather more than half the number of items in the chapter as a whole. This emphasis on personal experience is perhaps the strongest feature of British Quakerism in the twenty-first century. Friends seem to be more moved and influenced by statements that come from deep personal experience than by writings that seek to embody an ideal or would-be objective position.

The Draft made connexions with other earlier Quaker writings by including no less than four extracts from *Towards a Quaker view of sex*[6], the last one being from the 1964 revised edition. Only one of these passages specifically mentions homosexuality[7]. Otherwise they are concerned with matters that are universal, for example "Where there is genuine tenderness, an openness to responsibility, and the seed of commitment, God is surely not cut out. Can we not say that God can enter any relationship in which there is a measure of selfless love? – and is not every generalisation we make qualified by this?[8]"

There are eight extracts altogether in *Qf&p* that touch on homosexual experience. Two of them are taken from Gordon Macphail, the first dealing with AIDS, the second being an experience of God's love by himself and his partner in their homosexual relationship[9]. We can link these passages with the statement from Wandsworth Preparative Meeting in 1989, which begins:

We affirm the love of God for all people, whatever their sexual orientation, and our conviction that sexuality is an important part of human beings as created by God, so that to reject people on the grounds of their sexual [orientation] is a denial of God's creation... We realise that our sexual nature can be a cause of great pain as well as great joy. It is up to each one of us to recognise this pain, ... to reach out to others as best we can, and to reflect on our own shortcomings in loving others... We need to overcome our fear of what is strange or different, because we are all vulnerable; we all need love.[10]

Of particular interest is a quotation from the testimony concerning Jessie Gadsden (1912–90) prepared by Worcestershire & Shropshire Monthly Meeting[11]. It does not explicitly name her relationship with Mary Mills as lesbian, but the implication is there. Mary is referred to as Jessie's 'companion', and their relationship is termed 'a partnership'. Conversations with Friends from the area have assured me that the relationship was a lesbian 'marriage', though at the time the testimony was written some Friends were averse to being straightforward about it. During Jessie and Mary's lifetimes it was not unusual for two women to live together, nor was it necessarily the case that they were lesbian. It is ambiguous whether the testimony is celebrating a close friendship or a relationship with deeper dimensions. Friendship is certainly something to be celebrated anyway and is a characteristic of many couples whatever their sexuality.

Among other extracts that are significant for gays is one taken from a practical article by Arthur Hardy in *The Friend* of 1989[12]. It points out the need for parents to support and reassure their gay children and extend this feeling to their partners. Acknowledging the possibility that parents may be shocked by a gay person's revelation of his or her homosexuality, it goes on to emphasise the need for expressions of acceptance not only from family members but also from Friends and meetings.

The mood of Yearly Meeting when considering 'Close Relationships' was anxious and tense. It was not plain sailing, even under the reassuring care of Christine Davis and Jocelyn Burnell as Clerk and Assistant Clerk. Charles Lamb, of Limerick Meeting, had come from Ireland to try to prevent British Friends from straying from the straight and narrow in their attitude towards homosexuality. Other Friends were worried at the way in which marriage was liable to become a mere close relationship or steadfast commitment. There had been an opportunity for Friends to get some things off their chests in a large informal group led by Erica Vere rather than in a main session of the Yearly Meeting.

A comparison between the Draft and the texts printed in *Qf&p* graphically illustrates the changes that had to be made. A minute was made in session that removed the problem of what status the extracts on sexuality had. It was a compromise, but one that was appreciated on all sides. The minute found its place as 22.19 in *Quaker faith & practice* and reads as follows:

> The Yearly Meeting has struggled to find unity on this [the subject of sexuality], which comes so close to the personal identity and choices of each one of us. We are still struggling for the words which will help us, so that we may come to know the balance which allows us both to deal with the personal tensions of our own response to sexuality and also to see ourselves as all equal in the sight of God.
>
> The extracts in this section are an anthology of the evolving experience of Friends and meetings. While our own [individual] experience does not identify with every extract, we recognise, in love, the Friend whose experience is not our own. We pray for ourselves, that we may not divide but keep together in our hearts.

The section on 'Marriage and steadfast commitment' contains eleven strong and useful passages on marriage and mutual love, including the passage from the testimony concerning Jessie Gadsden. It then goes on to a completely new section headed 'Celebrations of commitment'. This opens with a piece by Don Grimsditch and Doris Mitchell-Grimsditch about renewing their marriage vows forty years later in a Quaker meeting for worship. The final extract, by Alison Davis and Mark Hughes, focuses on the couple's decision to have a 'celebration of commitment' rather than a 'marriage'. Framed, as it were, by these two clear, fully aware and joyful statements we have a struggling minute from Meeting for Sufferings in 1987:

> We recognise that many homosexual people play a full part in the life of the Society of Friends. There are homosexual couples who consider themselves to be married and believe that this is as much a testimony of divine grace as a heterosexual marriage. They miss the public recognition of this as a religious ceremony even though this could have no legal significance.
>
> We have found the word 'marriage' difficult but we are clear that we have a responsibility to support all members of our meetings and to uphold them in their relationships. We can expect that some committed homosexual couples will ask their meetings for a celebration of their commitment to each other. Meetings already have the means whereby meetings for worship can be held for this purpose but we recognise that many find this a difficult matter. The acceptance of homosexuality distresses some Friends.
>
> Meetings may well find it easier to consider this matter in connection with specific relationships rather than in the abstract, but we believe that meetings may be helped if something of the exercise of this meeting is shared with them.[13]

Both *This we can say* and *Quaker faith & practice* were published in 1995. The former was the product of a coherent small group, though it nonetheless had its own internal struggles. The group wanted to push the Society of Friends forwards. We wanted the Society to come face to face with the messy realities of contemporary life, which the traditional Christian positions seemed ill equipped to tackle adequately. *Quaker faith & practice* had a different and larger remit in attempting to crystallise the Society's position at a time of great social change. The Revision Committee had worked over a similar length of time to the *This we can say* group, and the process continued in the actual Yearly Meeting sessions.

At different points over the forty-odd years of struggle from *Towards a Quaker view of sex* to the acceptance of *Quaker faith & practice* in 1994 some Friends have felt obliged to resign their membership. We do not know whether the resignations were motivated solely by disagreements about sexual matters or whether the latter were just symptoms of a greater disquiet. The numbers are probably small. The annual tabular statements about membership do not support the idea that there were mass resignations. Like society at large, the Religious Society of Friends in Britain was also changing.

7

Celebration

After Meeting for Sufferings had made it clear in 1988 that Monthly Meetings had the power to arrange meetings for worship to celebrate committed relationships, though without any validity in law, a number of gay and lesbian couples requested such occasions. The first British Quaker gay celebration of commitment took place at Oxford Friends Meeting House on 22 July 1995. The two men involved were Jon Brown and Steve Hope. Other such celebrations followed. It is worth noting, however, that Jon and Steve applied to Oxford Meeting in April 1994 asking them to appoint a meeting for worship to celebrate and affirm their relationship, and that it took about sixteen months of discussion before Oxford Friends could agree to do so.

One of the problems for gay and lesbian couples requesting a celebration of their commitment to each other was that it was not taken for granted in the way that heterosexual couples could assume. It would not be a happy or appropriate event if there were Friends in the Monthly Meeting who were uncomfortable or actually opposed the union. How could one know in advance whether Friends would welcome a celebration? The couple would need to be very sure of themselves and their position within the relevant Meeting. The meeting for worship would be a public declaration of faith. Despite these drawbacks several celebrations took place, but they were held in the main in large urban areas. Although a degree of publicity attached to them through notices in *The Friend*, many monthly meetings had no direct experience of their spiritual and emotional impact on all present at the celebrations. As is the case generally with homosexuality, personal acquaintance and experience make a tremendous difference in how individuals react.

The biggest breakthrough, however, came with changes in civil society. For the general stability and cohesiveness of society gays and lesbians needed equality with straights on employment issues, job security, inheritance rights, pensions and so on. Pressure from trades unions, civil rights activists and the European Union led eventually to the 2003 Civil Partnership Act, which permitted the civil registration of same-sex relationships granting legal parity with marriage. Many Quaker lesbian and gay couples took advantage of this provision, as announcements in *The Friend* testified. Often the couples concerned had been living together for decades, demonstrating the solidity of their mutual commitment.

From the Quaker viewpoint the civil registration of same-sex couples has the drawback that it is resolutely secular. Any religious or spiritual element is prohibited. In consequence two couples in my area meeting (Manchester and Warrington), one male and one female, requested a meeting for worship on a separate occasion. Sean and Alistair had had a civil partnership registration in January 2006, but the meeting for worship did not take place until 16 September in order to ensure that relatives and friends could be present. The meeting took place in Mount Street Meeting House, Manchester, and was attended by around 250 people who had come from far and wide, including Northern Ireland, to wish them well. The two men were overwhelmed by the occasion and each ministered. Sean's father and Alistair's mother signed the certificate as witnesses. Sean and Alistair had actually been together for about twenty years.

A similar, but smaller celebration took place at Warrington Friends Meeting House on 19 May 2007 for Angie and Janet. Both of these occasions were warmly supported by local Quakers as well as friends, relatives and work colleagues. It was very important for the area meeting, as all four Friends whose partnerships were celebrated were (and continue to be) very active within their local meetings and the area meeting as a whole. For everyone concerned the two celebrations were full of love and support.

Events such as these match the desires of the individuals concerned, but they do not furnish a pattern to fit everybody. Many Quaker gays and lesbians have partners who are not Quakers. They may wish to celebrate their civil partnerships in other ways and possibly with very little fuss. The important thing for Quakers is to be flexible and kind to each other.

The absence of a spiritual dimension from the civil partnership registration provided by the State was troubling to many gay, lesbian and straight Friends. If equality of treatment and esteem were the goal, then gay, lesbian and straight Friends ought to have an identical expectation in the registration of partnerships. In September 2007 Quaker Life set up a Working Group on the Recognition of Partnerships under the auspices of Britain Yearly Meeting. In the course of its deliberations this group called a conference at Woodbrooke consisting of representatives from area meetings, registering officers, members of the Quaker Lesbian and Gay Fellowship, members of the Quaker Committee for Christian and Interfaith Relations and other interested Friends. It met from Monday to Wednesday, 2–4 June 2008. Representatives came from as far afield as Aberdeen, Carlisle, Exeter, Wales and the south coast of England as well as the London area. The aim was to discuss possible proposals in the autumn to Meeting for Sufferings.

It was a carefully focused and well organised conference. As a necessary background Christine Trevett gave a richly informative and challenging presentation on the theology of marriage from

Biblical times onwards, with special reference to the early Quaker understanding. Michael Hutchinson, Assistant Recording Clerk and General Secretary of Quaker Life, provided some historical background on Quaker involvement in issues to do with homosexuality. In small groups of six the participants were confronted with four topics for consideration: (1) the variety of partnerships that could be recognised by Friends and how; (2) the theology of marriage and other partnerships; (3) the terminology to be used; (4) the role of registering officers.

In both the plenary sessions and small groups there was a huge amount of personal input. The large proportion of lesbians and gays present made their dissatisfaction with the present situation very clear, mainly through examples from their own experience. Many had encountered astonishing levels of ignorance among Friends in their meetings, as well as among the wider public, about what it means to be homosexual. A lot of educational work was necessary. These voices were heard frequently, and the level of emotion was high among speakers and listeners alike. But there were also voices on the other side of the exchange of views. The word 'marriage' being extended to gay and lesbian couples was a distressing prospect for some Friends, but it was very difficult for them to articulate the precise reason why. One participant was so upset by the flow of discussion that she left the conference before it ended. The conference had not been designed to produce minutes or reach particular conclusions, but rather to explore the issues. Many of us were not sure whether we had actually helped the Working Group in their task, but were assured that we had. The conference generated a very powerful experience. Several participants said it was the best they had ever attended. The eloquent pressure of those who wanted progress could, however, have been inhibiting for those with a different viewpoint.

The Quaker Life Working Group submitted a report and recommendations to Meeting for Sufferings on 1 November 2008.

Recognising the varied experience that Quakers up and down the country had had of celebrations of same-sex partnerships, the Group first of all recommended that some common practice should be achieved in the Yearly Meeting before any legislative change were to be envisaged. The Group had looked carefully at different ways in which equality of treatment for gays and straights could be achieved in regard to committed partnerships. It decided that, at the present time, it would be inappropriate to recommend the surrender of our present authority to conduct Quaker marriages, an authority hard fought for in the past. In the future registering officers could well be involved in preparing and conducting the events, however called. The Group agreed that terminology was an issue and pointed out that 'marriage' was used in three different senses in Chapter 16 of *Quaker faith & practice* (1995). On the use of 'marriage', 'partnership' or 'union' the Group made no recommendation.

Meeting for Sufferings included the whole of the Working Group's report to Quaker Life in its own minute and sent the matter on to Yearly Meeting, which considered it at a residential Yearly Meeting held at the University of York, 25 July–1 August 2009.

Nobody could say that this issue came out of the blue. It had been well aired among British Friends in committee work, talks, small groups and a conference. The Agenda Committee of Yearly Meeting also made careful preparations. With approximately 1,700 Friends of all ages present at a joint occasion of Yearly Meeting and Summer Gathering there needed to be a variety of opportunities for both individuals and groups to look at the subject before the crucial Yearly Meeting sessions. The Quaker Lesbian and Gay Fellowship organised a special interest group in which people were given a variety of scenarios with tricky judgements to be made about hypothetical problems. On the Monday morning Colin Billett, convener of the Quaker Life Working Group, spoke persuasively to the report on 'Committed Relationships'.

On the Tuesday there were four separate presentations, each about ten minutes long, illustrating the diversity of close committed relationships. The first came from Jenny Shellens, speaking in a forthright and determined way on behalf of herself and her partner Alice Lynch. The second speaker was Owen Claxton-Ingham, who told us about the lengths that he and his partner Rob had gone in order to have a gay Quaker marriage (in Canada). They had, before being married, adopted a girl and a boy. The third presentation was from a mid-life heterosexual couple who had fallen in love after supporting each other in bereavements and then wanted a Quaker marriage. The final speaker was Sean Hughes, whose partner Alistair Gault stood supportively behind him. Sean spoke about his attempts to train as a Roman Catholic priest, his heterosexual marriage and divorce, then meeting Alistair, whose background was Church of Ireland, being together for twenty years and having a civil partnership and a meeting for celebration at Mount Street. The cumulative impact of these four intensely personal stories was enormous. It was particularly telling because it was low-key, but deeply moving. Subsequent contributions in the afternoon from the body of the meeting were wholly affirmative, and they were many, both straight and gay. Susan Hartshorne pointed out that it was twenty-two years since she had put her concern for equality of treatment to Meeting for Sufferings and prepared a handbook of guidance to meetings about arranging for celebrations. The mood of Friends now was clearly for a move to equality before the law and for recognition of a spiritual dimension to celebrations of commitment.

At Yearly Meeting there was now time for reflection. The next day was devoted to excursions across much of Yorkshire. It was not until Thursday afternoon that we returned to the subject. A few Friends made it clear that they were not going along with the general flow that British Quakers should accept the principle of equality with regard to 'marriage'. One male Friend from West

Scotland (apparently not known to other Friends from that Area Meeting) spoke at length about the possibility that we were about to make a wrong decision with attendant negative consequences. In a manner not at all Quakerly he then left the meeting without listening to what anyone else said. The many contributions that followed were both diverse and supportive of the Yearly Meeting's leadings on equality. By the end of the session it became obvious that the sense of the meeting was ahead of what the clerks had anticipated. Friends did not want a cautious minute with more dithering. They wanted something more radical, not avoiding, but embracing the word 'marriage'. The clerk (Martin Ward) asked to be allowed to bring a draft minute to the Friday morning session, where, after the usual kind of Quaker niggles, it was accepted.

The Thursday session in particular was marked by a widespread feeling of excitement. There was a recognition that this was a historic occasion. It would have consequences that took time to deal with. Negotiations with the Government about possible legal changes would have to be set in train. We would need to explain our principled decision to other churches and faith groups. The Yearly Meeting decision was picked up by the media before it had been finally taken and officially announced, such being the power of individuals with mobile phones. The Yearly Meeting decision was picked up by the media before it had been finally taken and officially announced, such being the power of individuals with mobile phones. As soon as the decision was announced, Britain Yearly Meeting gave an interview to the Press Association and a press release was issued. *The Guardian* of Saturday, 1 August, carried both a brief press item and a leader page comment beginning: 'The decision yesterday by the Quakers to perform marriage ceremonies for gay couples was welcomed by campaigners such as Peter Tatchell as a trailblazing. But it is not the first time that the Religious Society of Friends has gone out in front.' It then mentioned Quaker involvement in abolition of the slave trade, prison reform and the treatment of the mentally ill. The leader ended as follows:

> The Quaker church will now ask the government to change the law to allow its officers to register same-sex partnerships as marriages. But legal recognition is secondary. The exploration of radical concepts is more important, as is the belief that there is good in everyone. As George Fox, the founder of the Quaker movement wrote, from prison of course: 'Then you will come to walk cheerfully over the world, answering that of God in everyone.'[1]

With *the Guardian* being the newspaper most widely read by British Quakers, its sentiments were greatly appreciated.

The Yearly Meeting recognised that it would have to engage with other churches to explain our decision. The Quaker Committee for Christian and Interfaith Relations (QCCIR), with Quaker theologians contributing, prepared a paper entitled 'We are But Witnesses' to explain the decision to other churches and faiths. It was sent to British church members of Churches Together in Britain and Ireland, and to members of the Interfaith Network. Comments were invited by that committee on the decision. The leaflet was distributed throughout the Yearly Meeting and made available on the internet. It was mostly taken up by members of the Yearly Meeting who were also seeking to understand the decision.

Much of what I've written in these chapters has had to do with small groups of concerned Friends as well as with official Quaker bodies at local and national level. But if Quaker concern with equality for gays and straights, homosexuals and heterosexuals, is to prove vital and real, it can't be left to gay Friends to carry. When a gay issue arises, especially locally, Friends too often turn to a gay or lesbian to deal with it. This is perhaps understandable, but it's wrong.

For many years now Manchester has had a Gay Pride March

(latterly just called Manchester Pride). It's held on the Saturday of the late August Bank Holiday weekend and is good-humoured, entertaining and great fun for participants and spectators alike. It's an opportunity for dressing up, clowning, playing music, singing, dancing and displaying banners of all kinds. The parade processes through over a mile of city-centre streets, loudly acclaimed by thousands of people lining the streets. On the fringe there are usually one or two very small groups of evangelical Christians and far right activists with their negative protests, but they are not allowed to disrupt proceedings. In 2008 gay and lesbian Friends and their supporters decided to join the march and display our Quaker banner. We had, as Manchester & Warrington Area Meeting, been running Quaker Quest programmes for several years in order to provide the general public with hands-on information about Quakerism. The fact that a number of young gays and lesbians had been attracted in this way challenged us to put ourselves on show at the Pride marches and to run an information stall, along with many other gay-friendly groups, at the principal venue in the Gay Village.

For many Friends walking in such an extravert march was not what they usually did, though they may have been in other demonstrations of a political kind in London and elsewhere. The public were high-spirited, uniformly friendly and cheered us on. We were one of the few groups with a mixed age range, including older (i.e. elderly) people. When we were making arrangements to participate in the march, the point was made that our concern for equality had to be demonstrated by straight Friends as well as gays and lesbians. This was amply clear in the 2008 march and the two that have taken place since. What is more, Friends enjoyed themselves and what they saw of the march. Individual Friends have been active in similar events in other parts of the country, especially Brighton and London.

The Yearly Meeting decision of 2009 marked over fifty years

of Quaker involvement in the process of working towards homosexual equality in marriage. It was not the end of the story, however. Discussions with the Westminster Government about the legal situation are ongoing, and the Equality act of 2010 now makes civil partnerships on a religious premises possible (if a faith body wishes). It is clear that there has been a huge social change in attitudes towards homosexuality, ranging from persecution and punishment in the 1950s to acceptance and celebration in the early years of the twenty-first century. As with many other social changes, one can't claim that it has been total, but the equal rights that have been won are enshrined in law and enforced. Individual attitudes and feelings are perhaps not as easy to change. It is likely that some, fed by ignorance or prejudice, will persist as anachronisms lacking all credibility.

The Yearly Meeting decision of 2009 was so whole-hearted and joyful that some Friends may assume that the path towards that decision was easy. Let us remember that on a number of occasions Meeting for Sufferings was reluctant to walk on the path of what, with hindsight, we can call progress. The writers of letters to *The Friend* (not necessarily representative of the views of the average Quaker) expressed disquiet, distress and annoyance as well as calm judgement and encouragement from 1960 onwards. Friends, like other people, needed to have their eyes opened to both the riskiness and the ordinariness of homosexual lives. Social changes do not happen overnight; they are the result of numberless small actions coming together and moving forward. Quakers in Britain have been part of this change, from time to time among the leaders of it, but on the whole we have sat on the sidelines or been ignored by the secular majority. The story of Quaker involvement is still worth telling, though, because it shows how small groups, working together under concern and prepared to devote the necessary time, made a difference to the resolution of an important area of social injustice.

Bibliography

Altman, Dennis, *Homosexual oppression and liberation*. London: Angus & Robertson, 1973).

Babuscio, Jack, *We speak for ourselves: experiences in homosexual counselling*. London: SPCK, 1976; revised edition 1988.

Bailey, Derrick Sherwin, *Homosexuality and the western Christian tradition*, London: Longmans, 1955.

Banks, John and Martina Weitsch, eds., *Meeting gay Friends*. Manchester: Friends Homosexual Fellowship, 1982.

Barnes, Kenneth, *The creative imagination*, Swarthmore Lecture. Friends Home Service Committee, 1960.

Blamires, David, *L'Homosexualité telle que nous la vivons*, trans. Philippe Giron. Paris: Centre du Christ Libérateur, 1980.

Gillman, Harvey, *A minority of one*, Swarthmore Lecture. Quaker Home Service, 1988.

Gorman, George, *The amazing fact of Quaker worship*, Swarthmore Lecture. Quaker Books, 1973.

Grey, Antony, *Quest for justice: towards homosexual emancipation*. London: Sinclair-Stevenson, 1992.

Hodges, Andrew and David Hutter, *With downcast gays: aspects of homosexual self-oppression*. Pomegranate Press, 1974.

Quaker faith & practice. London: The Yearly Meeting of the Religious Society of Friends (Quakers) in Britain, 1995.

This we can say: Talking honestly about sex. Reading: Nine Friends Press, 1995.

Towards a Quaker view of sex (revised edition). London: Friends Home Service Committee, 1964.

Speaking our truth: a plain Quaker's guide to lesbian and gay lives. QLGF, 1993.

Endnotes

Preface

1. 'Writing Homosexuality from the inside', *Friends Quarterly*, (vol. 38, no. 3).

Towards a Quaker view of sex

1. Antony Grey, *Quest for justice: towards homosexual emancipation* (London: Sinclair-Stevenson, 1992), p. 21.

2. *Report of the Committee on Homosexual Offences and Prostitution* (London: Her Majesty's Stationery Office, Cmnd. 247, reprinted 1968), p. 7.

3. Kenneth Barnes gave the 1960 Swarthmore Lecture with the title *The creative imagination*.

4. Joyce James, Testimony, YM 1996 Docs

5. Duncan Fairn, 1906–86, Testimony, QW 1986.

6. *Towards a Quaker view of sex* (revised edition) (London: Friends Home Service Committee, 1964), p. 41. The revised edition differs in many respects from the first edition of 1963, but there is no difference in the formulation of this extract.

7. George H. Gorman, 1916–82, Testimony, QW 1982.

8. Doris I. Eddington, 1897–1987, Testimony, QW 1987.

9. Stephen Thorne,1896–1968, Testimony, YM Proc 1969, the Recording Clerk.

10. Myrtle Radley, 1903–91, Testimony, QW 1994.

11. Hugh Doncaster, 1914–94, Testimony, YM Docs 1996.

12. See *Quest for justice: towards homosexual emancipation*, pp. 162–63.

13. *Towards a Quaker view of sex*, p.10.

14. *Towards a Quaker view of sex*, pp. 16–18.

15. Derrick Sherwin Bailey, *Homosexuality and the western Christian tradition* (London: Longmans, 1955).
16. 6 May 1960, p. 607.

Writing *Homosexuality from the inside*
1. *The Friend*, 20 August 1971, pp. 987–89.
2. Damaris Parker-Rhodes, 1918–86, Testimony, QW 1987.
3. Arthur White, 1913–95, Testimony, YM 1997 Proc.
4. Sections 40–44, covering four pages of foolscap.
5. p. 38.
6. Paragraphs 883 and 906.
7. Ted Randall, 1918–1986, Testimony, QW 1986.
8. Alfred Braithwaite, 1901–75, Testimony, QW 1975.
9. See John Banks, QLGF Newsletter, no. 129 (January 2011).
10. John Hartshorne, 1928–92, Testimony, QW 1992.
11. *Meeting gay Friends*, edited by John Banks and Martina Weitsch (Manchester: Friends Homosexual Fellowship, 1982).
12. Dennis Altman *Homosexual oppression and liberation* (New York: Outerbridge & Dienstfrey, 1971).
13. *L'Homosexualité telle que nous la vivons* (Paris: Centre du Christ Libérateur, 1980).
14. See David Blamires, 'Writing in the furtherance of ministry', *Friends Quarterly* (October 2007), pp. 344–51.

Friends Homosexual Fellowship
1. Dennis Altman, *Homosexual oppression and liberation* (New York: Outerbridge & Dienstfrey, 1971).
2. Jack Babuscio, *We speak for ourselves: experiences in homosexual counselling* (London: SPCK, 1976; revised edition 1988).
3. Roger C. Wilson, 1906–91, Testimony, QW 1991.
4. *The Friend* (1 September 1978).

5. *The Friend* (30 January 1981).

6. No publication details given, but late 1981 or 1982.

7. Audrey Wood, 1908–98, Testimony, QW 1998.

8. For more details about Charlotte Wolff see Antony Grey, *Quest for justice: towards homosexual emancipation* (Sinclair-Stevenson, 1992), pp.151–52.

9. Andrew Hodges and David Hutter, *With downcast gays: aspects of homosexual self-oppression*, (Pomegranate Press, 1974).

10. The subject was dealt with at considerable length in an article by Chuck Fager entitled 'Quaking over gay rights: what really happened in Wichita', *The Straight Creek Journal* (14 July 1977).

11. *Speaking our truth: a plain Quaker's guide to lesbian and gay lives* (QLGF, 1993).

Towards Recognition

1. *Quaker faith & practice*, (1995), 22.45.

2. *The Friend* (1987), p. 880.

3. Yearly Meeting 1989 met in Aberdeen and had several weighty matters before it, principally the Inter-Church Process and the Yearly Meeting's decision whether or not to join the Council of Churches for Britain and Ireland. There was no session specially designated to discuss the recognition of same-sex relationships.

4. Harvey Gillman, *A minority of one*, (Quaker Home Service, 1988), pp. 61–62.

5. *A minority of one*, p. 62.

6. *A minority of one*, pp. 62–63.

7. *A minority of one*, pp. 64–65.

HIV/AIDS and 'Clause 28'
1. Gordon Macphail, 1956–91, Testimony, QW 1993.
2. *Friends Quarterly*, July 1990.
3. Ecclesiasticus or Sirach 6: 15–16.
4. *Friends Quarterly*, October 1988.

This we can say
1. *Friends Quarterly*, October 1988.
2. *This we can say: talking honestly about sex* (Reading: Nine Friends Press, 1995).
3. *Quaker faith & practice* (London: The Yearly Meeting of the Religious Society of Friends (Quakers) in Britain, 1995).
4. Paras. 481 – 510.
5. Para 569.
6. *Quaker faith & practice*, 22.13, 22.15, 22.18, 22.49.
7. *Quaker faith & practice*, 22.15.
8. *Quaker faith & practice*, 22.18.
9. *Quaker faith & practice*, 22.17; 22.29.
10. *Quaker faith & practice*, 22.16.
11. *Quaker faith & practice*, 22.40.
12. *Quaker faith & practice*, 22.69.
13. *Quaker faith & practice*, 22.45.

Celebration
1. http://www.guardian.co.uk/commentisfree/2009/aug/01/in-praise-of-the-quakers?INTCMP=SRCH